BLACK
AND
EPISCOPALIAN

THE STRUGGLE FOR INCLUSION

T0131294

BLACK
AND
EPISCOPALIAN

THE STRUGGLE FOR INCLUSION

GAYLE FISHER-STEWART

FOREWORD BY KELLY BROWN DOUGLAS

CHURCH
PUBLISHING
INCORPORATED

Copyright © 2022 by Gayle Fisher-Stewart

All rights reserved. No part of this book may be reproduced, stored in a retrieval system, or transmitted in any form or by any means, electronic or mechanical, including photocopying, recording, or otherwise, without the written permission of the publisher.

Unless otherwise noted, the Scripture quotations are from New Revised Standard Version Bible, copyright © 1989 National Council of the Churches of Christ in the United States of America. Used by permission. All rights reserved worldwide.

Church Publishing
19 East 34th Street
New York, NY 10016

Cover design by Tiny Little Hammers
Typeset by Rose Design

Library of Congress Cataloging-in-Publication Data
Names: Fisher-Stewart, Gayle, author.
Title: Black and Episcopalian : the struggle for inclusion / Gayle Fisher-Stewart.
Description: New York, NY : Church Publishing, 2022. | Includes
    bibliographical references.
Identifiers: LCCN 2021038023 (print) | LCCN 2021038024 (ebook) |
ISBN 9781640654785 (paperback) | ISBN 9781640654792 (ebook)
Subjects: LCSH: African American Episcopalians. | Race relations--Religious
    aspects--Episcopal Church--History.
Classification: LCC BX5979 .F57 2022 (print) | LCC BX5979 (ebook) |
    DDC 283/.7308996073--dc23
LC record available at https://lccn.loc.gov/2021038023
LC ebook record available at https://lccn.loc.gov/2021038024

To my nieces, nephews, and grands,
let no one stop you from being who God has created you to be.

Until the lion can speak, the story will always glorify the hunter.

—African Proverb

I've spent my entire life proving that I belong in elite white spaces that were not built for Black people. . . . I decided I didn't want to do that anymore.

—Nikole Hannah-Jones

CONTENTS

FOREWORD

What is the connection between the Anglican/Episcopal Church, the cotton fields of chattel slavery, and Nat Turner's uprising? As Gayle Fisher-Stewart seeks to answer this question, she takes us through the complicated history of the Episcopal Church when it comes to the very sin of white supremacy that gave birth to the cotton fields and precipitated Turner's rebellions. Her search gives way to the stark pronouncement that the Episcopal Church is "racist to the core." Behind this unflinching pronouncement, however, is a nuanced truth-telling about this "racist core." It is, on the one hand, a core that makes peace with an "anti-Black" society that cast Black people as inhuman. For Fisher-Stewart, there is no better example of this than the wealth that Episcopal congregations accrued from their as well as their members' direct ownership of Black bodies.

On the other hand, the Episcopal Church's racist core is further seen in its obsequious neutrality when it comes to contentious racial issues. No greater example of this, Fisher-Stewart notes, is the Church's "point of pride" in not "officially" splitting "over the issue of slavery during the Civil War." Essentially, as Fisher-Stewart makes clear, the Church's esteemed unity laid bare the fact that "the Episcopal Church refused to take any position on the issue of slavery."

Overall, Gayle Fisher-Stewart paints a picture of the Episcopal Church—from its earliest beginnings in Jamestown, Virginia, to its nine provinces today across the United States, Latin America, and the Caribbean—that is too often beholden to its Anglican origins as the "via media" (middle way). For what becomes painfully clear in this portrait of the Episcopal Church are the compromises that it makes with Black freedom, Black dignity, and Black lives in an effort to alienate no one and thus maintain harmony. In many respects, this book lays bare perhaps another truth of the Episcopal Church: a commitment to unity frequently supplants the concern for justice—at least when it comes to race. And, what is made abundantly clear in the story Fisher-Stewart tells, such a concession is not benign. Rather, it plays itself out on Black bodies through policies of exclusion, paternalism, and even hostility. Even more disturbing is that such via media–like concessions too often render the church complicit in the sometime fatal disregard of Black lives in wider society.

This book, however, does not stop with history. Rather, the history gives way to hard theological/faith decisions regarding being "white or Christian," and more pointedly being "Black and Episcopalian." This latter decision is at the heart of this book, as it is a story not only of how the Church has or has not included Black people but also whether or not Black people should want to be included.

It is in this way that this book is about Gayle Fisher-Stewart's personal dilemma, but not one she faces alone. As she wrestles with the dilemma of being both Black and Episcopalian, Fisher-Stewart essentially engages in a dialogue with other Black Episcopalians, lay and ordained, who are likewise wrestling. We hear their stories, their everyday experiences, of the Church in "their own words." Yet, with all that is revealed, in all of its brutal honesty, what is most striking is that Fisher-Stewart and those with whom she speaks choose to remain in a church that has been described as "racist to its core."

In the final analysis, though a stark picture of the Episcopal Church is revealed, this book is not an unrelenting diatribe. Rather, it is a passionate call for the Church to live into its faith and its better self. It is a hard truth-telling from a priest who loves her church. It is a book that brings us just a little bit closer to "Becoming the Beloved Community." For as Gayle Fisher-Stewart makes clear from the very beginning of the story she tells, "the only way toward the Beloved Community, as is the call of the Episcopal Church, is to start by telling the truth—the complicated, hard, sometimes uncomfortable truth." *Black and Episcopalian: The Struggle for Inclusion* is a story of truth that Becoming Beloved Community demands.

The Very Rev. Dr. Kelly Brown Douglas
Episcopal Divinity School at Union Theological Seminary
September 2021

BEGINNING WORDS

When we cannot tell the truth about our past, we become trapped by it.

—James Baldwin

It was 1996, and I was driving south from Washington, DC, down Interstate 95. I was going to Wakefield, Virginia, to visit a friend who lived on a six-acre farmette. South of Richmond and east of Petersburg, Virginia, I drove, passing fields and farms, watching the dirt turn from dark brown to whitish-gray. The crop was something I had not seen before: green leaves with a small flower on top; the stalks held a white ball. I turned into my friend's driveway and found myself between two fields of this strangely beautiful plant, but these fields were different. Some plants had been defoliated, which made it easier, I was to learn, for the mechanical combines to pick the plants' bounty. Then I realized I was in the middle of a cotton field. The white balls were the cotton bolls. Some fields had already been shorn of their prize by the combines. My friend came up beside me.

"Cotton?" I asked.

"Yep, we grow cotton here."

As I surveyed the harvested fields, I saw some cotton on the stalks and on the ground. I looked at my friend, who is white, and said, "We would not have been permitted to leave all that cotton behind."

She looked at me, and an uncomfortable half-smile came across her face. "You're probably right."

Today, combines strip the cotton from the plants instead of the gnarled, broken, and wounded Black hands that did the backbreaking work all day, from "see to can't see." Cotton. A little more than one hundred miles from Washington, DC, I dug up a plant with the cotton still on its branches and brought it home. Every day, I look at that cotton plant and think of my people, their lives in this country then and our lives in this country today.

Later that day I continued exploring. I turned left out of the driveway, and less than fifty yards down the road I saw a county line marker that read "Southampton County." Southampton County, Virginia, site of

Nat Turner's 1831 rebellion: Black people fighting against their enslavement. The next day, we took the ferry across the James River and drove to Williamsburg, not far from Jamestown, the first permanent English settlement in this country. In Williamsburg, we stopped in Bruton Parish Church, a former Anglican, now Episcopal church, that was established in 1674 and is still in operation. I could not help but feel a connection between cotton (the economic system), Nat Turner's uprising, and the Anglican/Episcopal Church. But how could it feel so current?

To hate a person or a group of people because of the color of their skin is a choice, an irrational choice. People choose to hate; therefore, they can choose to stop hating. Hatred—particularly racial hatred in the church—is an affront to God. I'm not concerned with why people hate, why they look at me and people who look like me and hate, because any reason is an excuse. The question I continue to struggle with is this: Can I be a part of a church or a denomination that acknowledges that racism is systemic, that racism is in its very DNA, and does not garner every single resource to confront and eliminate it? To say, "all have sinned and fall short of the glory of God" (Rom. 3:23) and not repent does not cut it anymore.

As Episcopalians, we understand that when we read the Bible, we must consider the context in which the people who initially wrote it lived and the context of those who later interpreted it.[1] We understand that people before us did not have as much knowledge and information as we have today. When we read scripture, what we might see as prescriptive could just as easily be taken as an observation. Yes, all of us have sinned, but we can control some sins, and the sins that denigrate God's people ought to be at the top of our list for elimination if we are true to our claim to follow Jesus. We don't have to wait until the Lord's return for things to be made right—especially if we care about the future of our children.

My grandmother was churchy. She was in the church every time the doors were open. She was one of the church ladies who sold chicken and crab cake dinners out of the back door of her house to support the church. In her later years, she became the "Mother of the Church." She was a member of the "sit-down" choir: the choir for the elders of the church.

---

1. Christopher L. Webber, *Welcome to the Episcopal Church: An Introduction to Its History, Faith, and Worship* (New York: Morehouse Publishing, 1999), 56–57.

She prayed over every one of the multitude of pills she took each day. She was deeply religious, and she was a realist. My grandmother didn't suffer fools, in or out of the church. If the church wasn't doing what it was called to do, she'd leave. Over the years, she was Methodist, African Methodist Episcopal Zion, African Methodist Episcopal, and nondenominational. If the church wasn't working to make life better for others, then it ceased to expect her support. This was a woman who, when she decided paying rent didn't make sense, purchased bricks every week until she had enough to build her house, the home she lived in until she died. She purchased the bricks, and she built—not *had* built, but *built*—her house herself, alongside her minister, who was a contractor, a minister who was what we call bivocational. Even working alongside her pastor, she had a saying, one of many that has stayed with me since her death twenty years ago: "Shit or get off the pot." This sainted woman actually used that phrase and said it with emphasis. In other words, don't waste time; don't waste her time; don't waste resources. If you're not going to do something, if you're not going to give it your all, move over, get out of the way, and let someone else do what you won't.

That's how I feel when it comes to the Episcopal Church and racism. Racism in the Church reminds me of the story of Peter and the disabled beggar at the Beautiful Gate in Acts 3.[2] Peter and John were going to the temple to do what folks did at the temple. They encountered a disabled man who was brought by neighbors or relatives and placed at the gate to beg for alms. We can imagine the man at the gate every day. As people came and went, they either stepped over him or ignored him on their way into the temple to make sacrifices and ask God to tell them what they should be doing. If we look at the Church today, people come to get their praise on, to worship God, to ask for guidance in how they should live their lives, all the while stepping over or ignoring the beggar on the steps. Like the people going in and out of the temple, we fail to see that God has already given us our assignment. Racism is the beggar on the steps. However, we fail to see; we don't want to see what we are called to do. Yet we pray:

O God, you made us in your own image and redeemed us through your Son: Look with compassion on the whole human family;

---

2. Acts 3:1–10.

take away the arrogance and hatred which infect our hearts; break down the walls that separate us; unite us in bonds of love; and work through our struggle and confusion to accomplish your purposes on earth; that, in your good time, all nations and races may serve you in harmony around your heavenly throne; through Jesus Christ our Lord. Amen. ("For the Human Family," Book of Common Prayer, 815)

The prayer "For the Human Family" feels otherworldly. First, it says to do things "in your good time," to which we must ask, "When will that be?" Black and Brown people continue to labor under the evil of racism. There is another out in the prayer: "all nations and races may serve you in harmony around your heavenly throne." This is end-times talk, where it seems that nothing will happen until Jesus's second coming; therefore, we have no power to change anything in the present tense.

"Becoming Beloved Community: A Long-Term Commitment to Racial Healing, Reconciliation, and Justice" is the Episcopal Church's vision that "frames a path for Episcopalians to address racial injustice and grow as a community of reconcilers, justice-makers, and healers."[3] In it, we find another "out": "Becoming the Beloved Community will take more than one three-year cycle of the Church's life. *It will take more than our lifetimes.*"[4] This is another excuse for those who don't want to work for justice, who believe that ending racism is not what they are called to do, who believe that systemic racism does not exist. And yet, as one who walks around under the threat of death because of the skin color God gave me, I do not find this to be satisfactory.

Let's tell the truth: the Anglican Church—the Church of England—and then, after disestablishment, the Episcopal Church have dealt with the race issue with questionable results. Consider these records from Bruton Parish in 1767, the church in Williamsburg:

Baptism of Slaves
Bruton and Middleton Parish Records
1662–1797, page 59

---

3. The Episcopal Church, "Becoming Beloved Community . . . Where You Are: A Resource for Individuals, Congregations and Communities Seeking Racial Healing, Reconciliation, and Justice," updated July 2020, *https://www.episcopalchurch.org/wp-content/uploads/sites/2/2021/02/BBC-Becoming-Beloved-Community-Where-You-Are_2020.pdf*, 2.

4. The Episcopal Church, "Becoming Beloved Community," 3, emphasis mine.

April the 5th Day: 1747

Gift Negroe Infant belonging to John Bryan Jur.

Nancy & William Belonging to Mr. Benjamin Waller[5]

The church records the baptism of the enslaved who belonged to its members. There is more in the parish records. In 1767 "Thomas" was born to "Molly," and "Molly" belonged to Bruton Parish.[6] This parish owned at least two enslaved persons. The Church owned enslaved persons. How many more Anglican/Episcopal churches owned human beings? How many more did Bruton Parish own? We cannot be afraid of where an investigation of history will take us. In the practice of becoming beloved community, we are called to tell the truth about our churches and race.[7]

A 2021 Racial Justice Audit conducted by the Episcopal Church acknowledges that systemic racism is embedded in the Church. "Since the church's founding, Episcopalians of color have in one way or another struggled to have the institution and its leaders recognize their dignity, power and gifts," the report reads.[8] Since the 1950s, resolutions have been passed at General Convention addressing racism; however, when do we get serious with the business of eliminating this sin that damages our relationship with God and each other?

For the Church, freedom must be more than a song we sing or a flag we wave. It must begin with the cross that calls us to claim freedom and to free our Church and nation from America's original sin—white supremacy. We long for the day when our Church might be free to become what we have aspired to be, a true Church following a crucified and risen Lord and witnessing to God's just future.[9]

"The Black body was never meant to be free." The Very Rev. Dr. Kelly Brown Douglas said those words in the aftermath of the police killing of

---

5. *Bruton & Middleton Parish Register 1662–1797*, Bruton Parish, Williamsburg, VA, accessed July 29, 2021, *www.heritagecenter.brutonparish.org*.

6. John Vogt, ed., *Bruton Parish, Virginia Register, 1662–1797* (Athens, GA: New Papyrus Co., 2004), 52. (Available at the Alexandria Library, Alexandria, VA, noncirculating collection).

7. The Episcopal Church, "Becoming Beloved Community," 3.

8. The Mission Institute and the Episcopal Church, "Racial Justice Audit of the Episcopal Church: Executive Summary," January 2021, *https://www.episcopalchurch.org/wp-content/uploads/sites/2/2021/04/RR-Racial-Justice-Audit_Exec-Summary_ENG.pdf*.

9. Kelly Brown Douglas, Winnie Varghese, and Stephanie Spellers, "Speaking of Freedom," July 6, 2020, video, 12:31, *https://www.youtube.com/watch?v=WX94bgC7dBM&t=21s*.

Baltimore, Maryland, resident, Freddie Gray.[10] Her words spoke to the past and the future of Black life in this country. When the "20 and odd negroes" were off-loaded at Port Comfort (now Hampton), Virginia, they were being traded for supplies. While they were not technically enslaved, they were not free. They might have been held in the same conditions as the indentured European servants, but they were not free. They were already dehumanized because they were being traded for things. There was no plan for manumission at some future time. They were in a state of un-freedom. They could not get back on the *White Lion*, the *Jesus*, or the *San Juan Baptista*—the ships that would bring millions of Africans to the Americas and head back home to Africa. They were not free without having to be told they were not free. Their color marked them as not free. They were the fly in the buttermilk, and the church, the Christian church, as Jemar Tisby writes,[11] was complicit in the creation and maintenance of that state of not being free.

Our color means that our lives can come to an end at any moment, not by disease or accident, or natural death, but by state-sanctioned violence; therefore, we are un-free. As activist Kimberly Jones has proclaimed, when your skin color is your weapon, you are always armed and dangerous. We are not free. We are not free, even in the Church because there are still some churches, including the Episcopal Church, where you might be tolerated, but you are not truly welcome, even if you are the priest—the white church's Black priest.

"How does it feel to be a problem?" It is difficult to discuss race in this country without at least referring to Dr. W. E. B. Du Bois. How does it feel to have two warring bodies inside you struggling to be free?[12] How does it feel to always see yourself through the eyes of those who would have you un-free? Du Bois wrote that the color line was the problem at the beginning of the twentieth century,[13] and that problem still exists. It is only by the grace of God, a great High God, a Creator God, that this entire country has not been burned to the ground. Why is it that

---

10. Kelly Brown Douglas, "Kelly Brown Douglas on Expanding Narrative of Race," April 25, 2015, interview by WBAL-TV 11 Baltimore, video, 3:09, *https://www.youtube.com/watch?v=fblH5AnMmAY*.

11. Jemar Tisby, *The Color of Compromise: The Truth about the American Church's Complicity in Racism* (Grand Rapids, MI: Zondervan, 2019).

12. W. E. Burghardt Du Bois, *The Souls of Black Folk*, 12th ed. (Chicago: A. C. McClurg and Co., 1920), 1–15.

13. Du Bois, *The Souls of Black Folk*, 1.

rules, regulations, laws that deny the humanity of people are so easy to obey, while those that lift up the humanity of all people are fought tooth and nail? For the church to be part of all of the -isms and phobias that shame the image of God revokes the church's right to call itself the body of Christ.

What is three-fifths of a human being? Certainly not fully human. Less than human? What is less than human? That is how we are memorialized in the founding document of this country, even though the Constitution has been appended with the Thirteenth and Fourteenth Amendments. Our humanity still does not matter. We have not mattered since we stopped being beasts of burden that created the wealth the 1 percent of people in this country enjoys. Our lives didn't matter during slavery any more than a wagon, or a pig, or a horse. A Black man ascending to the highest position in this country did not make our lives matter. President Barack Obama's election actually has brought white backlash. Those who once hid behind white sheets are now free to share their racist propaganda through print, electronic, and social media. They felt free to storm the United States Capitol building on January 6, 2021, erect nooses on the Capitol grounds, and stand fully armed with their arms around police officers to take selfies.

In 2015 I watched with tepid anticipation as Michael B. Curry was feted by the Union of Black Episcopalians at the DC Armory the day before he was to be consecrated as the first African American to be elected presiding bishop of the Episcopal Church. The sonorous singing voice of Dr. Sandra T. Montes took us to church. The cultures were all mixed in the worship service. It was upbeat, it was spiritual, it was the picture of Revelation 7:9 but here on earth—right here, right now. It was Black Church on steroids. And yet I knew, just as it was with the election of Barack Obama, the election and consecration of Michael Curry was not an indication of a postracial country or a postracial Church. Racism is real. Racism is ever-present. Racism is deadly. Watching the Church party on that day was a "yes, but" experience. Yes, today we can forget, we can imagine a different country, a different Church . . . but tomorrow the real world, apparently one beyond the reign of God, will return in all its deadly habituations.

Tell the truth: too often the church and religion do not include; both exclude. If you don't believe right (orthodoxy); if you don't do right (orthopraxy); if you don't pray right, look right, dress right, have sex right; if you don't sing the right hymns, use the right sacred text, adhere to a particular liturgy, or hold fast to ancient doctrines, you are excluded. If you don't believe Jesus is the only way, you are excluded. The history of the church has been one of exclusion: division over who Jesus was, division over one line in the Nicene Creed, division over whether we are justified by faith alone, division over whether the pope is infallible, division over how we do church, division over whether Black people were (are) human. We have continued to fracture the body of Christ with the many denominations, nondenominations, and interdenominations. We are divided because we Christians think we have the truth that no other faith tradition has. Within the Christian faith, several claim that mantle of the only one true church and see all others are pretenders to the throne.

It is always difficult when generalizations are used to discuss groups of people or when a system is critiqued, but there are no apologies here. Every single white person in this country benefits from the racism[14] that has existed since the decision was made by white Christians to enslave Blacks and to use the Bible to justify their racism. My apologetic is in the mold of Henry McNeal Turner, Marcus Garvey, Ida B. Wells, Jarena Lee, and Pauli Murray, all of whom worked to force the Church to see itself as it is: racist to the core. Kehinde Andrews tells us that we must decolonize our knowledge; we must decolonize our minds about how to worship a God who is the God of all and not just of whiteness.[15]

Whatever we need to do as Black people—the face of exclusion in the Episcopal Church—we need to do. However, whatever, and whomever we need to worship to keep our minds, souls, and bodies intact, we need to worship, and we don't need anyone's permission to do so. Call it syncretism, call it blending, call it religious fluidity; call it whatever you want. Pray to the God, a god, no god, if it keeps us from doing as American Christianity, the American Christian church, has attempted to do to us: destroy us. We need to do whatever keeps our souls and bodies intact. What might be orthodox to whites just might not be orthodox to Blacks. We don't need white folks' permission to thrive.

---

14. Whites generally do not have to think about race, that race could keep them from owning a home or receiving a loan. They move into Black communities without wondering if they will be welcome. They usually don't think about whether the schools their children attend will have the necessary resources or if they will be welcome in a church of their choice.

15. Kehinde Andrews, *The New Age of Empire: How Racism and Colonialism Still Rule the World* (New York: Bold Type Books, 2021).

At the entrance of the library at Virginia Theological Seminary, an Episcopal seminary in Alexandria, Virginia, this quote from William Sparrow, a nineteenth-century dean of the seminary, is chiseled into the stone at the door: "Seek the Truth; come whence it may, cost what it will."

The truth concerning racism in this country and the church is not complete; it's partial, just the tip of the iceberg. We don't like complete histories in this country, especially if that history shares an ugly side of the church or the country. When a more complete history that does not gloss over racism is presented, it is met with cries of revisionism—especially if whiteness is not given top billing in all things good and noble. I, for one, did not receive the full picture of how the Anglican/Episcopal Church was complicit in the enslavement and continued degradation of Blacks when I took the class History of the Episcopal Church at Virginia Seminary in 2014. How many before me left with an incomplete picture of the role their Church played in the dehumanization of Africans in this country? How many since 2015? Becoming Beloved Community compels us to tell the truth, and that truth will hurt because it implicates us all. If we tell the truth, we will have to admit that the Episcopal Church "perpetuated white supremacy and racist practices and beliefs, and . . . it continues to benefit from, participate in, and perpetuate(s) racism to this day."[16]

In 2015 the Very Rev. Dr. Kelly Brown Douglas was invited to speak at the historically Black Calvary Episcopal Church in Washington, DC. As she mesmerized the packed audience for four hours discussing her book, *Stand Your Ground: Black Bodies and the Justice of God*,[17] she told of the complicity of the Christian church in the debasement and dehumanization of Black people in this country. She told of a plantation theology (my term), a plantation eschatology that told the enslaved that if they were good slaves and obeyed their masters, one day they would get to heaven. This heaven, like life on earth, would be segregated. There would be a fence down the middle of heaven separating the Black heaven from the white heaven, and Blacks could peek through a hole in the fence and catch a glimpse of the white heaven.

Western Christianity has been and continues to be largely complicit in the dehumanization of Black bodies. Many people will go down to the

---

16. The Mission Institute and the Episcopal Church, "Racial Justice Audit of the Episcopal Church."

17. Kelly Brown Douglas, *Stand Your Ground: Black Bodies and the Justice of God* (Maryknoll, NY: Orbis Books, 2015).

grave defending their white Jesus. There are whites who believe that God is white and heaven is for white people—at least the white side of heaven is for white people. White racism gave birth to the Black Church. Born out of oppression, born out of racism, born of a people who also struggled with a white Jesus and then learned much later that "God is a Negro,"[18] the Black Church stood in opposition to Western Christianity. Had it not been for white Christian racism, there would be no Black Church or Black congregations in white denominations. Whites helped create the Black Church in America.

What does it mean to be Black in a country that is steeped in anti-Blackness? What does it mean to be part of a faith tradition that has anti-Blackness as a value? What does it mean to be Black in the Episcopal Church, born out of the Church of England, which, if it did not birth slavery, was its midwife and breathed life into it, and which also has anti-Blackness in its DNA?

Can I be Black and Episcopalian?

I am Black, and I am a member of the Episcopal Church. Toward the end of 2020, I spoke at an adult forum for a colleague's church about my book, *Preaching Black Lives (Matter)*. I received an email that indicated the session had been well received; however, one comment had a different tone:

> Churches are not Black or white! You are a racist! The color of your skin is irrelevant! Humans are humans! All the same! "As a Black woman, as a Black priest"—identifying yourself by the colour of your skin—just treat everyone the same and the issues will disappear! ALL LIVES MATTER! Stop dividing!

Can I be Black and Episcopalian? In this time of Black Lives Matter and civil unrest as a result of the killing of Black people by the police, the increased incidents of racial hatred stoked by the rhetoric of the former president, and the continuing backlash to a more inclusive history of race being taught in our public schools, how is it to be the only Black person or among a few Blacks in a congregation that is overwhelmingly white? And what are the resources available to clergy and laypeople through the church—or are there any resources? Is there the belief that if you are ordained, you ought to be able to thrive in any congregational situation?

---

18. As proclaimed by AME Bishop Henry McNeal Turner. Gayraud S. Wilmore, *Black Religion and Black Radicalism: An Interpretation of the Religious History of African Americans*, 3rd ed. (Maryknoll, NY: Orbis Books, 2003), 152.

As discussions have highlighted, many clergy, Black and white, find it difficult to preach about race or Black Lives Matter in predominantly white congregations. Rather than face backlash, many just don't broach the topic. Others have attempted to preach race and have had members walk out in the middle of the sermon, send emails threatening to leave or withdraw their financial support, or "greet" them at the end of the service and chastise them for preaching politics.

As for laypeople, several have indicated they have yet to hear a sermon on race. For these laypeople, the names of George Floyd or Breonna Taylor or any other Black person killed by the police or who has faced racism has not been mentioned from the pulpit where the priest is white. The question, then, is why do you stay? Why stay at a church that appears to have no real interest in dealing with the dehumanization of Black people?

This book is a journey, a journey to wholeness in which we first explore the struggle of Blacks to be fully included in the Episcopal Church. Then we move to the question of which comes first—Black or Christian? It might seem a strange question; however, many Black folk have struggled with the question and have decided that Black trumps being Christian. Then, there is the Black Church. Born out of the crucible of racism, there is no way in these few pages to cover the Black Church in all its fullness. What is the Black Church, and how does it continue to be a safe space against the racism so present in the white church? Every organization requires that its members and adherents change in the image of the organization. The church is no different. We call it formation. Yet the question is formation as what—disciples of Christ or white Episcopalians? Formation or education, in the words of bell hooks, is political because it is rooted in the antiracist struggle. It is a counterhegemonic act in which we resist every strategy of white racist colonialism.[19] Along this journey of history, lament, and hope, I had the privilege of interviewing Black clergy and lay members of the Episcopal Church. They shared how they have navigated the whiteness of the Episcopal Church. These interviews, all of which were more than one hour in length, have been compressed, and quotations are found interspersed between the chapters. I wish I could have used the interviews in their entirety because they, too, provide a window into the lament, despair, and hope that is part of the Black experience in the Episcopal Church. We end with "Sending Words" that include

---

19. bell hooks, *Teaching to Transgress: Education as the Practice of Freedom* (New York: Routledge, 1994), 2.

recommendations for the Episcopal Church to rid itself of the racism that is embedded in its DNA so that it can live up to its mantra, "The Episcopal Church Welcomes You." Ultimately, I am answering this question for myself: Can I be Black and Episcopalian, and if not, then what? Like the old hymn says, this is my story, this is my song.

In Their Own Words

It began as a simple Facebook post, asking for Black volunteers to speak about their experience either serving or worshiping in predominantly white Episcopal churches. I was also interested in hearing from folks who had served or attended historically Black parishes. What follows, having condensed over fifteen hours of interviews, is just a glimpse of how Black clergy and laypeople navigate the white space that is the Episcopal Church.

Male Clergy

The majority of my white members, just from a numbers standpoint (I would say 5 to 10 percent), have adopted children from Africa: one adopted an Ethiopian boy, or they have adopted Black children. Either both parents are white and the kids are Black or one spouse is Black and the other is white. Our biggest growing edge has been either white parents with Black children or multiracial parents who then have, you know, multiracial children who are biologically their own. The white parents I talk to, with children who are Black, say their families are in white spaces all the time—school, primarily white neighborhoods, at home is white— and they wanted a place where their children could see themselves and see Black leadership on the altar, and also become friends with other children who look like them.

Female Laity

However we define our Blackness, it is important that we keep the space safe for Black people. Since the Black Church has been a place of safety and support and where we learn our leadership skills and how to deal with the public, it is important to maintain that. We know our acolytes have to be trained in an exact way to do their duties so if they're out in the diocese, people don't say, "Oh, they don't know what they're doing." So we have to overtrain. Everybody who was going to be part of a diocesan event is overtrained, so they know what to do better than the white folks know what to do. We had to make sure that the clergy leadership understood that they had a very important role when white folks would come in and say, "Oh, well, we want this kind of music." And we say, "You know, we do this kind of music. We also do Taizé, and we do the traditional Anglican hymns; we do all of that. If you need to have that all the time, you need to find another church." We also needed to have clergy understand their role as the clergy of a congregation that, while welcoming all people, want to maintain their Blackness. We did have clergy who wouldn't like the spirituals or the gospel music or clapping hands when the bishop was there, which called for a conversation. We know that being an Episcopalian is joining a predominantly white denomination, but you're not going to put us in that box. We're not going to be that all-white congregation. So, if you need to have that all-white congregation, as our clergy you need to ask the bishop to move you someplace else.

Female Clergy

There have been times when I've been invisible. For example, while in seminary speaking with a white faculty member, a young, white female student came up and just started her conversation, and the faculty member began talking with her, and when she left, he turned back to me. I had to tell him, that's not good to do when you're speaking with a Black person. I've also found that I've been asked to either join an all-white staff or apply to be called as rector for an all-white church because they needed some color. I've also been in some places where there wasn't another Black person for miles around. I've been asked because a church really wanted to change, wanted to come into the twenty-first century as it pertains to racial issues, and I've also had to remind them that I was not there so they could check the appropriate boxes. At one church where I was rector, people actually left because I was called.

Female Clergy

I stayed in predominantly white contexts throughout my career. I went where the bishop sent me after graduation and ordination. The congregation called itself diverse, but it was really white. There were some people of color: Black, Asian—some. But what we really dealt with was my sexual orientation. My rector didn't want to tell anyone. He said, "I don't want it to be the first thing you tell them." It was during the time when Gene Robinson was consecrated. All things became contentious. What I figured out about myself is that I've worked really hard to be liked, and it hurt very deeply. I feel like I wasn't liked. Almost twenty years later, I still haven't really shaken that. But I think the way I coped in predominantly white spaces is to figure out how to make them like me so they wouldn't treat me like shit.

Female Laity

When an African American became rector, the atmosphere was different; there was covert stuff, there were microaggressions. I was surprised at the racism. I must give [the rector] credit for holding her ground and doing her job well and with dignity. I never asked her how I might have helped. She and I never talked specifically about racism and how it was affecting both of us. I regret that we never had that conversation. I thought about [another rector] who said, "At what point does it become too much for a congregation when too many Black folks show up?" Just my family [being the Black members] didn't matter, but some members did have problems with [the Black rector] being the authority.

CHAPTER ONE

THE STRUGGLE FOR INCLUSION IN THE EPISCOPAL CHURCH

Is it possible for Black people to maintain integrity and identity within a "white" church?

—John T. Walker, Bishop of Washington

What does it mean to be a Christian witness in a racist church?

—Rev. Van S. Bird, of Philadelphia

The Episcopal Church had probably done less for Black people than any other aggregation of Christians.

—W. E. B. Du Bois

I do not think it would have been very strange if the colored race, after it had been freed, should have refused to follow the white people's God. It shows a higher order of intelligence and an acute discernment in the African race to have distinguished the good from the evil, in a religion that taught all men were brothers, and practiced the opposite.

—The Rt. Rev. Henry Codman Potter, Bishop of New York

We usually skip from slavery to the Civil Rights Movement of the 1960s and skip over everything in between. We talk about Absalom Jones and then skip to Jonathan Myrick Daniels because we don't want to talk about the church's complicity with racism and slavery and want to pat ourselves on the back and only tell what we think are the good parts.

—Crusty Old Dean, "The Episcopal Church's Lost Causism"

An apology without action is manipulation.

—Rose Hudson-Wilkin, Bishop, Church of England

The late bishop of Washington John Walker asked, "Is it possible for Black people to maintain integrity and identity within a 'white church'?" His question names the struggle in the Episcopal Church since Blacks first came under the control of the Anglican Church in colonial Virginia in 1619. Updating the question for today, it might be, "Why would any Black person want to be Episcopalian if the history of the denomination were fully known?" There is the tendency to go around in ignorant bliss, focusing on the beauty of the liturgy while failing to accept that systemic racism is a reality whose continued trauma is four hundred years in the making. We worship in incense-laden somnambulism with some applying the balm of "heaven's my home" and believing that suffering somehow gets us closer to God, all the while knowing that for many African Americans, Christianity has lost its power. They find little comfort in knowing that Jesus was killed by the empire and that the empire could also end their lives.

In the words of Azariah D. A. France-Williams, "The Church of England was the dominant ecclesial force during the transatlantic slave trade."[1] The search began in earnest. We were preparing for the first session in the diocese's antiracism training. I agreed to develop the section on race and the Episcopal Church. We wanted to tell the story from the very beginning, not after the Revolutionary War and disestablishment of the Church of England. Yes, the Episcopal Church apologized for its complicity in slavery and segregation in 2006; however, I needed to show a closer connection with the Church and the beginning of slavery in this country—not just being complicit, but active involvement in the debasement of Africans in America. After all, in the Virginia colony the Anglican Church and the government were one and the same. To be a member of the vestry, a man also had to be a member of the Church of England. Church attendance was required. If one lived in Virginia, membership in the Church of England was automatic. Today, as in colonial times, France-Williams writes, "The Church of England is both the Cross and the Crown."[2]

In my search for information, I began with the text used in seminary to teach the history of the Episcopal Church. After all, if the history of the Church is part of the curriculum for seminarians, the entire story, would

---

1. A. D. A. France-Williams, *Ghost Ship: Institutional Racism and the Church of England* (London: SCM Press, 2020), 38.

2. France-Williams, *Ghost Ship*, xviii.

be told, wouldn't it? But, just like the history of slavery in this country, the history of the Episcopal Church was missing key details. Everyone began with the arrival of Africans in Jamestown in 1619 as if it had been some kind of pleasure trip.[3] As I was preparing for ordination, a colleague had given me his archival copies of *An Outline History of the Episcopal Church* and *The Episcopal Church and Freedom*. In the former, the year 1619 was memorialized with these words:

> In 1619 delegates from the several counties were sent to form, with the Council, the General Assembly, the first representative legislative body for the colony. That Assembly made the laws for the colony, including the religious life of the people.[4]

What seemed to be of importance to the author was that the discipline of the Church was to be used to repress "excess in apparel" by the wives of churchmen that could result in public fines.[5] Nowhere was slavery mentioned. The second source, a pamphlet reprint of the 1955 *Anglican Theological Review*, regaled how the Episcopal Church contributed to the maintenance and extension of freedom. The writer, M. Moran Weston of the National Council (later renamed Executive Council), dealt primarily with the General Conventions of 1922, 1949, and 1952. From the report submitted by the Joint Commission on Social Reconstruction, the discussion on equality provided the following:

> The first step in establishing equality for all is a vigorous effort, expressed in legislation, to secure full civil rights for every citizen of the United States. The Church must demand, both corporately and through its individual communicants, that the brotherhood of man and the equality of all in the sight of God, be best recognized by the nation, immediately and fully.[6]

Equality for the nation as opposed to equality in the Church was the focus. This is shown in words such as "all men are created equal," and words have no power on their own. They must be backed up with action.

---

3. Robert W. Prichard, *A History of the Episcopal Church: Complete through the 78th General Convention*, 3rd rev. ed. (New York: Morehouse Publishing, 2014).

4. Frank E. Wilson, *An Outline of the Episcopal Church* (New York: Morehouse-Gorham, 1952), 3.

5. Wilson, *An Outline of the Episcopal Church*, 3.

6. M. Moran Weston, "The Contribution of the Episcopal Church to the Maintenance and Extension of Freedom," *Anglican Theological Review* (April 1955): 7.

The search continued to another book, *Essays on Segregation*, written in 1960. Six white Episcopalians, all male—four rectors, one retired bishop, and a layperson—concluded that segregation was not opposed to the gospel of Jesus Christ and that any Episcopalian who advocated for integration would have to deal with that decision on judgment day.[7] But still, nothing on the origins of slavery and the Episcopal Church. I was beginning to believe there was no direct connection between the Anglican Church in America and slavery when "twenty and odd negroes" were brought to the colony of Jamestown until I came across a book I used to teach the course Race and the Criminal Justice System at the University of Maryland. It was this legal text that gave life to my hunt for the connection between the Anglican/Episcopal Church and the founding of slavery in what would become the United States.

There is always discussion about whether the first Africans in the colony of Virginia were indentured servants or enslaved. It does not matter. Indentured or enslaved, the Africans were not free to embark on the next ship and return to Africa. In the book *In the Matter of Color—Race and the American Legal Process: The Colonial Period*, the jurist A. Leon Higginbotham assessed how the law became a tool to enforce injustices based on color, and he provided the clear connection between the Anglican Church as an institution that more than implicates it in the enslavement of Africans.[8] Until disestablishment of the Church after the Revolutionary War, the Church was in lockstep with the government. Church wardens and vestries acted as agents of the state. For example, the following is from the 1691 statute (Act XVI):

> And it is enacted that if any English [i.e., white] woman being free shall have a bastard child by a Negro, she shall pay fifteen pounds to the *church wardens* and in default of such payment, she shall be taken into possession by the church wardens and disposed of for five years and the amount she brings shall be paid one-third to their majesties for the support of the government, one-third to the *parish* where the offense was committed and the other third to the informer. The child shall be bound out by the *church wardens* until he is thirty years of age. In case the English

---

7. T. Robert Ingram, ed., *Essays on Segregation* (Houston: St. Thomas Press, 1960).

8. A. Leon Higginbotham, *In the Matter of Color—Race and the American Legal Process: The Colonial Period* (Oxford: Oxford University Press, 1978).

woman that shall have a bastard is a servant she shall be sold by the church wardens (after her time is expired) for five years, and the child serve as aforesaid.[9]

While this particular law is from 1691, the House of Burgesses, which would later become the General Assembly, was formed in 1619. To be a legislator, the men had to be members of the Church of England. With the establishment of select vestries in the parishes (churches), there was a comingling of functions when slavery was enacted in 1640. Both the vestries and the House of Burgesses were populated with slaveholders. Perpetual slavery became a reality in 1640, when John Punch was sentenced to serve his master for his natural life after he and two indentured white men were convicted of the dastardly crime of seeking their freedom by running away. The court turned color prejudice into legal pronouncements.[10] With the Punch case, it was inevitable that slavery would develop unchecked in the colony and the Church.[11] Still, the connection between Christianity, the church, and enslavement was made clearer in 1667, when baptism, a right given by the Anglican Church, was ruled to have no effect on the state of bondage.

> 1667. Act III. Whereas some doubts have arisen whether children that are slaves by birth, and by the charity and pity of their owners made partakers of the blessed sacrament of baptism, should by virtue of their baptism be made free, it is enacted that baptism does not alter the condition of the person as to his bondage or freedom; masters freed from this doubt may more carefully propagate Christianity by permitting slaves to be admitted to the sacrament.[12]

A final nail in the coffin came in 1670, when the law was passed that further differentiated between Africans and the indigenous people in that "those imported into this colony by shipping, who 'shall be slaves for their lives,' and those who 'shall come by land,' who 'shall serve, if boys or girls; until thirty years of age: if men or women twelve years and no longer."[13] It is obvious that the Africans were "shipped" to the colonies.

---

9. Higginbotham, *In the Matter of Color*, 45, emphasis mine.

10. Higginbotham, *In the Matter of Color*, 28.

11. Winthrop D. Jordan, *White Over Black: American Attitudes Toward the Negro, 1550–1812* (Chapel Hill: University of North Carolina, 1968), 210.

12. Higginbotham, *In the Matter of Color*, 36–37.

13. Higginbotham, *In the Matter of Color*, 37.

The role of the Church in the business of slavery was made apparent by vestries purchasing the enslaved and attaching them to the glebes. The colony of Virginia was nothing but wilderness, and it was difficult to entice ministers from England to venture across the Atlantic. The vestry was responsible for calling a minister. Tobacco was the payment for any minister in the Anglican Church, and its cultivation required backbreaking work done by the enslaved.[14] To entice ministers to come to the colony, Anglican parishes were the first institutions in Virginia to own enslaved people who were acquired through donations from member enslavers and also through outright purchase.[15]

Always remembering that until disestablishment the Anglican Church and the House of Burgesses were one, permission was often given to the parishes to sell parish property and use the money to purchase enslaved persons. In one case, the General Assembly was very specific in how the money was to be used by one parish vestry. Ware Parish in Gloucester County was to purchase a number of enslaved persons, one-half of which were to be young females because females would increase the number of enslaved persons by giving birth. In another parish, Lynnhaven, the General Assembly directed the vestry to purchase enslaved persons for the specific task of reproduction, which would add to the value of the glebe.[16] The total debasement of Africans being complete, the Anglican Church in the colonies became the model for other denominations and colonies. James Blair, the highest-ranking Anglican official in the colony and the first commissary of the bishop of London, strove to have Virginia become a model of slaveholding for other denominations and colonies, and the Anglican Church provided the template.[17]

American Christianity and the Episcopal Church

In *White Too Long*, Robert Jones demonstrates how embedded white supremacy is in the DNA of American Christianity and how the evil that is white supremacy has undergirded the violence that has been visited on

---

14. William Webb and Anne C. Webb, *The Glebe Houses of Colonial Virginia* (Westminster, MD: Heritage Books, 2008), 28.

15. Jennifer Oast, *Institutional Slavery: Slaveholding Churches, Schools, Colleges, and Businesses in Virginia, 1680–1860* (Cambridge: Cambridge University Press, 2016), 14.

16. Oast, *Institutional Slavery*, 26.

17. Oast, *Institutional Slavery*, 29.

Black bodies since the first of them landed on these shores.[18] In converting them to an Anglican form of Christianity, the enslavers knowingly put themselves between God and the Africans and manipulated true Christian teachings for their personal and economic benefit.[19] As the latest Racial Justice Audit of the Episcopal Church delivers the bad news, which is not news to those of us who are not white, that systemic racism in the Episcopal Church is real, perhaps we are called to follow the advice of France-Williams and "build a new house and urge those in the burning house to escape." France-Williams is referring to the comment made by Martin Luther King Jr. concerning integration in a conversation with the singer and activist Harry Belafonte:

> I've come upon something that disturbs me deeply. We have fought hard and long for integration, as I believe we should have, and I know we will win, but I have come to believe that we are integrating into a burning house. . . . Until we commit ourselves to ensuring that the underclass is given justice and opportunity, we will continue to perpetrate the anger and violence that tears the soul of this nation. I fear I am integrating my people into a burning house.[20]

The question that must be asked is whether the continued quest for full equality and opportunity for Blacks in the Episcopal Church is "integrating into a burning house" (as Martin Luther King Jr. feared) and whether the current structure of the Church should be dismantled and a new Church formed—one that is based on the gospel of Jesus Christ. The Racial Justice Audit reported, "Episcopalians of Color have been, in one way or another, fighting and demanding that the institution and white leaders recognize their dignity and gifts since the establishment of The Episcopal Church."[21] Systemic racism exists, and it was the intent of this report to examine the effects of systemic racism and how systemic racism is maintained. The report also mentions that a racial audit was conducted

---

18. Robert P. Jones, *White Too Long: The Legacy of White Supremacy in American Christianity* (New York: Simon & Schuster, 2020), 3, 5.

19. Shawn M. Copeland, *Enfleshing Freedom* (Minneapolis: Fortress Press, 2010), 42.

20. France-Williams, *Ghost Ship*, 26–27.

21. The Mission Institute and the Episcopal Church, "Racial Justice Audit of Episcopal Leadership," January 2021, *https://www.episcopalchurch.org/wp-content/uploads/sites/2/2021/04/RR-Racial-Justice-Audit-Report_ENG.pdf*, 12.

in 1991 and concludes that "a clear pattern of institutional racism existed at every level of the Church."[22] In 1994 the House of Bishops issued a pastoral letter that said that racism was totally inconsistent with the gospel and that it must eradicated.[23] Since this is the reality of the Episcopal Church, why do Black Episcopalians stay? What is the benefit of staying in a burning house?

Harold T. Lewis, the eminent historian of the Episcopal Church, offers three reasons Black Episcopalians remain in the Church in spite of the trauma that constant fighting for recognition of their humanity causes:

- Black Episcopalians have distilled the essential message of the gospel from the corrupted and co-opted message of the Church and white Christianity;
- Black Episcopalians believe they have an inherent right to remain— a four-hundred-year history—and they have unique gifts to offer a Church that needs to face its racism and become the body of Christ; and
- Black Episcopalians believe they are in a unique position to be agents for change if barriers are no longer placed in their way.[24]

To this list Lewis adds,

> Black Episcopalians have consistently held the Church's feet to the fire and reminded it when its actions have been inconsistent with the principles it has espoused. In so doing, Black Episcopalians have consistently called the Church to be true to its catholic principles even when it had abandoned them, or had run the risk of abandoning them. [Further,] To most Americans the first image conjured up by the acronym WASP (white Anglo-Saxon Protestant) is the Episcopalian. . . . It is to this protestant context that Black Episcopalians have historically provided a catholic corrective.[25]

---

22. The Mission Institute and the Episcopal Church, "Racial Justice Audit of Episcopal Leadership," 12.

23. The Episcopal Church, "House of Bishops Pastoral Letter on Sin of Racism, March 1994," accessed July 29, 2021, *https://www.episcopalarchives.org/church-awakens/exhibits/show/awakening/item/111.*

24. Harold T. Lewis, *Yet With a Steady Beat: The African American Struggle for Recognition in the Episcopal Church* (Valley Forge, PA: Trinity Press International, 1996), 174–77.

25. Lewis, *Yet With a Steady Beat*, 7.

While Lewis makes excellent points, how many Episcopalians of any race know or understand what he has written? Where is this information, not only in the seminary experience but also in the formation process? Melva Wilson Costen posits there is sufficient evidence that African Americans today need to be freed from the white Christian church that remains a "pseudo-interracial, slave-worshiping environment."[26] A four-hundred-year struggle of Blacks in the Episcopal Church offers evidence of that environment.

Racism should be classified as a disease: a dis-ease of the soul, the mind, and the heart. The sin of racism makes people act irrationally, against their own best interests. For Anglicans, Africans were subhuman, just a little higher than animals, who "had no right to be instructed or admitted to the sacraments"[27] of the Church. This contradiction evidenced itself in multiple ways; two will be offered here. First, multiple laws were promulgated in colonial Virginia that banned sexual contact between the Africans and the English. These laws came after sexual contact had already occurred because the laws referred to "bastard" children born to such relations that were, often, instigated by the English. If the African is subhuman, not human, why would there be the desire for sexual relations unless there is another disease that made its way through the colonies? Second, why would you evangelize something that is subhuman? Why would you want to bring a subhuman to the Lord, even if it was for means of adding numbers to the church? Does this subhuman, less-than-human thing have a soul that is worth saving?

The Seed Is Planted

With the founding of the first permanent settlement in Virginia, the Church of England took root. The area between what is now Wilmington, North Carolina, and Charlottesville, Virginia, was part of the territory already named Virginia by Queen Elizabeth to honor herself. There were hardships and sufferings for those who made the voyage from England, beginning in 1606, to plant colonies and to get rich quick by finding gold and silver in this so-called New World. For the nine hundred passengers who arrived at the mouth of the Chesapeake Bay in 1610 and

---

26. Melva Wilson Costen, *African American Christian Worship* (Nashville: Abingdon, 1993), 68.

27. Albert J. Raboteau, *Slave Religion: The "Invisible Institution" in the Antebellum South* (New York: Oxford University Press, 2004), 100.

then traveled further to the river they named the James, only 150 survived. Most died of disease and starvation. Later, with the formation of the Virginia Company, a private enterprise, hundreds of other colonists arrived. By 1614 the future of the colony was secured, and by 1619 that future was enhanced with the arrival of Africans and the establishment of the House of Burgesses as the first governing body in America.

Legislation that firmly planted the Church of England as the established church was enacted. Twice on Sunday attendance at divine service was mandatory. There were only three priests and two deacons at the time, and ministers were to be given one hundred acres of land called a glebe, with a fixed salary to be paid in tobacco.[28] This was the first act that legally established the Church of England in Virginia. Over the next few decades, the House of Burgesses gradually extended this religious establishment.[29]

In 1624 King James annulled the charter of the Virginia Company, and Virginia became a providence under the control of the monarchy, governed by officials appointed by the king. The House of Burgesses remained, along with a royal governor, with the goal that the Church of England be firmly established. The Church was organized with vestries through an act of the House of Burgesses. Ministers were nominated by the vestries and, after pledging their loyalty with conformity to the Church, were inducted by the royal governor. Tithes were collected by law, and no one could vote in the colony unless he was a member of the Anglican Church.[30] Local vestries, in addition to having responsibility for parish management, were also responsible for the collection of taxes and the administration of the local welfare system. Vestries functioned as a judicial arm of government, collecting fines and overseeing the punishment of colonists who violated civil laws. Vestries also tended to resist the royal governor's authority, and as a result, they were free to govern their parishes in any manner they chose,[31] which included the purchase of the enslaved.

It was within this context of racism and racist behavior that Anglicans evangelized Africans. It can be argued that evangelization was conditional

---

28. James Thayer Addison, *The Episcopal Church in the United States, 1789–1931* (New York: Charles Scribner's and Sons, 1951), 27–29.

29. David Hein and Gardiner H. Shattuck Jr., *The Episcopalians* (New York: Church Publishing, 2004), 11.

30. Addison, *The Episcopal Church in the United States*, 29.

31. Hein and Shattuck, *The Episcopalians*, 12.

since Africans were brought to the Church to ensure the continuation of slavery. Notice that the word *Church* was used as opposed to the phrase "brought to Jesus [or Christ]" because Africans were the only people who could determine whether they wanted to be one with Christ, even though they could be required to attend the enslavers' church and listen to a corrupted gospel message. While Africans worshiped with their enslavers, it is sometimes difficult to determine if the worship experience and pseudo-membership in the Anglican Church were voluntary. Africans who accepted the American version of Christianity made it their own; they Africanized Christianity. Even as Africans worshiped in the enslavers' churches or slave chapels when provided the opportunity, they snuck away to the hush harbors and worshiped as part of the invisible institution. The slave gallery often bears a negative connotation; however, putting aside the displayed racial self-oppression, George Freeman Bragg, a leader in the Black Episcopal Church, redeemed the slave gallery as an incubator of the Black Church:

> When one recalls the actual condition of the people brought hither from the barbarism of their native land, their ignorance and general unpreparedness in every particular for an intelligent participation in public worship, and, with abundant doubt entertained with respect to their capacity to assimilate and incorporate ideas, the slave gallery was a most convenient testing and proving ground for the unexplored ignorance thus brought close enough for experiment . . . for, out of the slave gallery came enlightenment, conversions, and Negro churches.[32]

While the slave galleries and the slave chapels were means of segregation, according to W. E. B. Du Bois, as the Black church before the official Black Church, these segregated venues provided the basis for the maintenance and preservation of the African half of the African American's identity. The invisible church of the enslaved represented all that remained of African tribal life and customs that the enslavers attempted to destroy. It was the place where the African traditions of family and tribe could be played out.[33] The fact that the Black Church survived and

---

32. George Freeman Bragg, *History of the Afro-American Group of the Episcopal Church* (Baltimore: Church Advocate Press, 1922), 38–39.

33. Du Bois, *The Philadelphia Negro*, 47.

thrived is a marvel in itself, according to Kyle Haselden: "The Negro Church stands as the symbol of the white Christianity's shame; yet it is a tribute to the power of the Gospel and to the faith of the Negro."[34] Haselden's observation is as germane today as it was when the slave galleries were in operation. Historically Black parishes today are both a symbol of the white Episcopal Church's shame and a tribute to the faith and tenacity of Black Episcopalians.

There was concern on the part of whites as to whether Africans or Blacks could actually be saved and go to heaven. Even as he advocated for the evangelization of Africans, the Episcopal clergyman and missionary Morgan Godwyn wrote, "What, such as they? What those Black dogs be made Christians? What, shall they be like us?"[35] Religious conversion and instruction were not a top priority for the Anglican Church. There was the fear that baptism would include freedom until Act III of 1667, which gave enslavers comfort that their sinful ways would not forever banish them to hell and damnation. They were free to enslave Christians. The main concern was the economic survival and physical safety of whites.[36] When there was instruction, it was to "cleanse and whiten the souls of heathens,"[37] language that was rife with white supremacy. However, the Africans were able to see through the hypocrisy of these so-called Christians and realized that regardless of what they were taught or what they heard, they would listen for the voice of the Great High God, who spoke directly to them with words of strength and empowerment.[38]

Black people were expected to accept their lot in this world, and if they were obedient, honest, and truthful, they would be rewarded after death. In a book of sermons and dialogues prepared in 1743 by a minister of the Protestant Episcopal Church in Maryland for use by masters and mistresses in their families, the enslaveds' response is:

> God will reward me; and indeed I have good reason to be content and thankful; and I sometimes think more so than if I was

---

34. Kyle Haselden, *The Racial Problem in Christian Perspective*, in Harold T. Lewis, *Yet With A Steady Beat*, 26.

35. C. Eric Lincoln, "The Development of Black Religion in America," *Review and Expositor* 70 (Summer 1973): 302.

36. Costen, *African American Christian Worship*, 20. See also, Higginbotham, *In the Matter of Color*, 36.

37. Costen, *African American Christian Worship*, 20

38. Costen, *African American Christian Worship*, 21.

free and ever so rich and great; for then I might be tempted to love and serve myself more than God. . . . But now I can't help knowing my duty. I am to serve God in that state in which he has placed me. I'm so to do what my master orders me.[39]

Disestablishment

When the War for White Freedom (otherwise known as the Revolutionary War) was over, the Church of England in the colonies was in disarray and faced a number of problems that grew out of the disestablishment of the Anglican Church, one of which was that taxes no longer supported the Church. With the ratification of the Bill of Rights, the first ten amendments to the US Constitution—and specifically, the establishment clause of the first amendment—the government could not require citizens to belong to any religion or to favor one religion over another. Previously, with colonies under English control, membership in the Anglican Church was assumed, regardless of a religious belief or actual membership in the Church. Mandated tithes to the Church were paid simply because of residency in the colony. This ended in 1791. The Church would have to fend for itself.

Another issue that troubled the soon-to-be Episcopal Church was the lack of a resident bishop to ordain ministers. Oversight by the bishop of London, which had minimally worked before the war, was no longer an option. What was desired was a church that still held to Anglican beliefs and doctrines but was truly American, however that might be determined. Factions emerged in the south, the middle colonies, and New England in an attempt to resolve issues that faced the disestablished church and to determine next steps that would result in the organization of the Protestant Episcopal Church. Clergy who rose to the top of the discussions were William White of Pennsylvania, Samuel Seabury of Connecticut, Samuel Provost of New York, Robert Smith of South Carolina, and William Smith of Maryland.[40] Connecticut elected Seabury as bishop in 1783, and he was sent to England to be consecrated, which failed because he would not swear allegiance to the king. He then went to Scotland, where nonjuror bishops were willing to consecrate him. He returned to

---

39. E. Franklin Frazier, *The Negro Church in America* (New York: Schocken Books, 1974), 19.

40. T. Felder Dorn, *Challenges on the Emmaus Road: Episcopal Bishops Confront Slavery, Civil War, and Emancipation* (Columbia: University of South Carolina Press, 2013), 4.

Connecticut in 1785 as the first American bishop and was followed by William White and Samuel Provost. In this tense environment, the three bishops had difficulty working together to unite for a consecration rite that was needed for the new Church to function. William White became the glue that would bring differing factions together so the infant American church could continue with the business of formalizing structure and governance.[41]

As the nuances and obstacles were worked out, a general convention was held in 1789, and out of it came a constitution, canons, and a prayer book. The Protestant Episcopal Church in the United States in America (PECUSA) was a reality. There were nine charter dioceses: Connecticut, Delaware, Massachusetts, Maryland, New Jersey, New York, Pennsylvania, South Carolina, and Virginia;[42] of course, slavery transferred from the Anglican Church to the Episcopal Church. As with any new organization, especially one born out of conflict and division, the Episcopal Church faced difficulties as it charted its way. Since it was still a slave-owning denomination, it continued spreading its corrupted form of the gospel to the enslaved purely because of the desire to win souls and to create a docile and less threatening workforce.[43]

The Non-schism Schism

For some reason, it seems to be a point of pride that the Episcopal Church did not officially split over the issue of slavery during the Civil War. The writings of Joseph Blount Cheshire in *The Church in the Confederate States: A History of the Protestant Episcopal Church in the Confederate States* shows a divide existed.[44] The reason the split was not formal was because the Episcopal Church refused to take any position on the issue of slavery. There was the belief and practice that the Church should not take a stand on any issue that was considered "political."[45] Not wanting a schism was more important than discussing the enslavement, degradation, and death of human beings held in bondage in society and by the

---

41. Dorn, *Challenges on the Emmaus Road*, 4–5.

42. Dorn, *Challenges on the Emmaus Road*, 6.

43. Dorn, *Challenges on the Emmaus Road*, 7.

44. Joseph Blount Cheshire, *The Church in the Confederate States: A History of the Protestant Episcopal Church in the Confederate States* (New York: Longmans, Green, 1912).

45. Addison, *The Episcopal Church in the United States, 1789–1931*, 192.

Church. The northern bishops did not want to upset bishops in the south, and the bishops in Virginia and South Carolina were extremely strong on that front. Anyone attempting to pass a resolution at General Convention would have been met with violent protest and resistance. If either House had been able to pass legislation condemning slavery, ecclesiastic secession would have been the result. The General Convention simply failed to act at all; it kept its head in the proverbial sand.

Two northern bishops had very close ties to those in the south: Bishop John Henry Hopkins of Vermont and Dr. Samuel Seabury of New York, the grandson of Samuel Seabury, the first Anglican clergyman ordained bishop for the Episcopal Church.[46] These two strong voices, among others, promoted the myths that the enslaved had consented to their status, which had been decreed by God, and that the New Testament did not forbid slavery. They encouraged whites to remember that the enslaved were "the happiest laborers in the world" and that the "Anglo-Saxon race is king; why should not the African race be subject?"[47]

The Church did split in 1861, when the southern bishops formed the Protestant Episcopal Church of the Confederate States of America, not over slavery but because the southern bishops could not be part of a church that was seen as being in allegiance with the so-called northern aggression. When secession of the southern states took center stage in 1860, there were sixteen bishops in the fifteen states where slavery was an issue; each of the southern states that left the union was led by a bishop. Bishops were also present in the four slave-holding states that remained in the union. When the Anglican Church was the established church, there was no separation between church and state; however, things were different for the Episcopal Church. The church and the state were not one. The bishops had to make decisions about how the Church would respond to an issue that was now seen as secular in nature but one that the Church had been involved in since the legalization of slavery in the colony of Maryland in 1663.[48] Rather than remain a unified church, the southern bishops went the way of the southern states that seceded; their allegiance was to the slave-holding states as opposed to the church. As evidenced by the Episcopal Church's unification after the war, it appears as though the

---

46. Addison, *The Episcopal Church in the United States, 1789–1931*, 193.

47. Addison, *The Episcopal Church in the United States, 1789–1931*, 194.

48. Dorn, *Challenges on the Emmaus Road*, 25.

Church did not care about or prioritize the enslaved, the church's freed members, or the thousands who would die in the Civil War.

While denying the *imago Dei* in the enslaved within their dioceses, and even as they were enslavers themselves, bishops continued to insist that enslaved persons be instructed in all things Episcopal. Stephen Elliott, bishop of Georgia, proclaimed, "There is no arrangement of worship so well-qualified as ours, to meet exactly the wants of our colored population. What they need is sound religious instruction."[49] In the diocese of South Carolina, the bishop was quick to falsely promote the benefit of religious instruction as being the creation of more docile enslaved persons and improved relations between enslaver and enslaved.[50]

Things were somewhat different in Virginia, where Bishop William Meade met with a group of Episcopalians (that included the well-known attorney and creator of the "Star-Spangled Banner," Francis Scott Key) in Washington, DC, in 1861 to discuss the emigration of Blacks to Africa. It was thought that the best way to deal with the enslaved within the country's borders was to have them voluntarily return to Africa; thus, the American Colonization Society was born, and twelve thousand free Blacks emigrated to Liberia, which gained its independence in 1847.[51] Meade and others believed that free Blacks were an ever-present reminder of freedom and therefore were a corrupting influence on enslaved Blacks and should be encouraged to leave. Others believed Blacks would never be accepted as full citizens with equal rights and that for their own protection, they should leave the country.[52] After the international slave trade was ended in 1808, enslavers preferred American-born enslaved persons because they had never known freedom.

Under Meade's episcopacy, he believed that the message of Jesus's gospel should be brought to the enslaved, yet he did not believe it was his mission or the church's mission to change the social order, that is, to end slavery. When Meade addressed the enslaved, he would tell them they should be thankful that they were born in this country and not in "some heathen land" where they would not receive the gospel, and that their heavenly freedom was more important than earthly freedom. He

---

49. Dorn, *Challenges on the Emmaus Road*, 27.

50. Dorn, *Challenges on the Emmaus Road*, 32.

51. P. J. Staudenraus, *The African Colonization Movement, 1816–1865* (New York: Columbia University Press, 1961), 27–28.

52. Dorn, *Challenges on the Emmaus Road*, 40.

preached a plantation theology that the enslaved were to accept the station that God allegedly intended for them and to "rejoice in the many spiritual blessings connected with it."[53]

Thomas Atkinson, the bishop of North Carolina, had different views about slavery. He emancipated his enslaved persons with the exception of "those who voluntarily chose to remain in the South."[54] Even though he manumitted his enslaved persons, he did not see a clear way for this country to abolish slavery. He considered Blacks to be "Christ's poor" to whom the Church was required to minister, although he did not believe in social equality. To minister to the enslaved was an obligation. William Whittingham was the fourth bishop diocesan for Maryland, and while he viewed Blacks as brothers and sisters in Christ, he never attempted to end the segregation that was prevalent in church services, where Blacks were confined to balconies or pews in the back of the church and were required to receive communion separately from whites. He was in favor of spreading the gospel to them and believed that if the Church did not, Episcopalians would be held responsible for permitting Blacks to "go down to the pit in brute ignorance."[55] Though they were not a true part of the church, even though baptized, Blacks were viewed as being mission; they were to have something done for them because of their degraded state. Atkinson was vocally concerned that other denominations were more attractive to Blacks and lamented that the Episcopal Church was not willing to make the necessary changes to its highly formalized service to meet the needs of Blacks. Finally, while he was against slavery, he also believed abolition to be a "great evil" because whites would not accept social equality, and the country was ill equipped to deal with millions of freed Blacks. He did ordain to the deaconate a Black man, Eli Stokes, in 1843, at St. James African Episcopal Church in Baltimore. Stokes left Maryland, organized St. Luke's in Connecticut, and was eventually ordained priest.[56]

What becomes apparent when studying the bishops in the enslaving southern states is that slavery presented an opportunity and obligation to save souls; however, when it came to the bodies of the enslaved, these bishops believed that slavery was not an evil institution they were called to

---

53. Dorn, *Challenges on the Emmaus Road*, 42, 46.

54. Cheshire, *The Church in the Confederate States*, 262.

55. Dorn, *Challenges on the Emmaus Road*, 58.

56. George Freeman Bragg, *Men of Maryland* (Baltimore: Church Advocate Press, 1914), 100.

speak against, although some did speak out against breaking up enslaved families. Ultimately, slavery was a civil institution over which the Church had no control, and therefore it was not within the purview of the Church to take any action to eliminate it.[57] Their failure to deal with the issue would not save their states or the Church, and their silence before the Civil War was solely to maintain church unity.

Some northern bishops might have opposed slavery but not enough to upset the relationships they had with their brothers in the south. The deafening silence, which migh even affect the church today, on issues of justice and equality that were seen as civil rather than theological issues led them to invoke the mantra that their job was only to preach the gospel and to save souls. But agreement on that would not save the fragile relationship between the bishops as the war encroached on the country, because each side saw their side as God's cause.[58] It can be said that no Episcopal bishop was a friend of Black people; the bishops' cause and concern was truly paternalistic. Their abject failure to see a contradiction between the gospel of Jesus and holding human beings in bondage was due to self-serving beliefs that if slavery was wrong, God would not permit it; that the institution of slavery had been with God's people since the beginning; and that to accept an abolitionist argument was to go against the Bible itself. To reject slavery was to reject the word of God.[59]

In the view of enslavers and white ministers of the gospel, the apostle Paul argued succinctly that the relationship between the enslaved and the enslaver was equal to that of a Christian and Christ.[60] Stephen Elliott, who was the first and only presiding bishop of the Protestant Episcopal Church of the Confederate States of America, defended slavery in his 1861 address at the Convention of the Protestant Episcopal Church in Georgia:

> We conscientiously believe it [slavery] to be a great mission-
> ary institution—one arranged by God, as he arranges all the
> moral and religious influences of the world, so that good may be

---

57. Dorn, *Challenges on the Emmaus Road*, 73–74.

58. Dorn, *Challenges on the Emmaus Road*, 88.

59. Dwyn Mounger, "History as Interpreted by Stephen Elliott," in Ted Booth, "Trapped by His Hermeneutic: An Apocalyptic Defense of Slavery," in *Journal of the Historical Society of the Episcopal Church* 87, no. 2 (June 2018): 160, 163.

60. Ted Booth, "Trapped by His Hermeneutic: An Apocalyptic Defense of Slavery," in *Journal of the Historical Society of the Episcopal Church* 87, no. 2 (June 2018): 165.

brought out of seeming evil, and a blessing wrung out of every form of the curse.[61]

Elliott also believed slavery had eschatological purposes, that the enslavement of the African would hasten Jesus's return. He warned the Church, this country, and other countries that to end slavery would interfere with God's plan and that slavery should be lifted up by Confederate generals as part of that plan.[62]

The failure to deal with the issue of slavery coupled with the desire to avoid a schism in the Church in fact resulted in what the bishops did not want—a schism. Although the bishops and others believed the myth that the Church should not be involved in political issues, it was the political issue of slavery and the war that caused the division they sought to avoid. South Carolina was the first state to secede from the Union on December 20, 1860, followed six weeks later by Alabama, Florida, Georgia, Louisiana, Mississippi, and Texas. The Confederate States of America was formed by representatives of these states on February 4, 1861. More southern states followed, and these states declared they belonged to an independent nation. The question that resulted in the breakup of the Episcopal Church was, How could members of the Confederate States of America continue to be loyal members of the Protestant Episcopal Church of America? Their Church became one that belonged to a foreign country that was also hostile. Their answer was to form their own church. The bishop of Louisiana, Leonidas Polk, who would later serve in the Confederate Army and die in action, and Bishop Stephen Elliott of Georgia called southern bishops and other diocesan representatives together in July 1861 for the purpose of forming an independent church. Discussions continued through October 1861, when a constitution, a carbon copy of the Episcopal Church's, was approved. On September 19, 1863, three days before the issuance of the Emancipation Proclamation, Bishop Elliott announced that the first General Council (as opposed to Convention) of the Episcopal Church of the Confederate States of America would meet in Augusta, Georgia, on November 12.[63] The schism was complete.

---

61. Booth, "Trapped by His Hermeneutic,"163.

62. Booth, "Trapped by His Hermeneutic," 174.

63. Addison, *The Episcopal Church in the United States, 1789–1931*, 195–96.

Robert E. Lee's defeat marked the end of the war. What were the Churches to do? Since there had been the desire to avoid schism in the first place, it was simply a matter of welcoming back the miscreant dioceses. While the bishops of Alabama, Georgia, and Mississippi were opposed to immediate reunion and represented the general sentiment of other southern bishops, the bishop of South Carolina was for permanent separation. The reunion was not easy.[64] In the midst of the turmoil, the Diocese of Alabama gave up trying to evangelize Blacks because "the ex-slaves would take neither their politics nor their religion from their former owners."[65]

The federal government adopted the position that the seceded states were still members of the Union regardless of their decrees and constitutions. The General Convention took a similar position and considered the seceded dioceses as merely absent.[66] It was a matter of semantics as to whether there was one or two Churches despite the evidence of two churches. The split was not over slavery as much as loyalty to the secular government.

Bishop John Henry Hopkins was presiding bishop. Prior to the General Convention of 1865, he personally wrote the southern bishops, invited them to attend, and promised that they would be warmly welcomed back into the fold. His sympathies lay with the South. He had a close relationship with Bishop Elliott of Georgia. As indicated previously, there was no hurry on the part of the southern bishops to return, at least not until the General Council of the Church of the Confederacy met to take action that took its lead from Bishop Elliott. A few southern deputies did attend the 1865 General Convention and were warmly received, setting in place the welcome mat for the return of all the southern dioceses.[67]

The schism that was not a schism was finally repaired in Augusta, Georgia, on November 8, 1865, when bishops and deputies of the Protestant Episcopal Church of the Confederacy acknowledged that the issue that resulted in the non-schism—the war between the states—no longer existed. The General Council resolved that the southern dioceses

---

64. Cheshire, *The Church in the Confederate States*, 215–31.

65. Edward Madal, *A Right to the Land: Essays on the Freedmen's Community* (Westport, CT: Greenwood Press, 1977), 77.

66. Addison, *The Episcopal Church in the United States, 1789–1931*, 198.

67. Addison, *The Episcopal Church in the United States, 1789–1931*, 198.

were free to withdraw from the current configuration and reunite with the Protestant Episcopal Church in the United States. Within a year, the Church had reconciled.[68] All was forgiven.

What to Do with the Negro?

After the Civil War, several Black parishes in the southern states attempted to affiliate with the dioceses in which they were located. Some bishops saw affiliation as a means of continued paternalistic control and favored taking the Black parishes under their oversight. The white laypeople objected. To have Blacks in the same diocese with their own white churches would be an affront to their whiteness, even though Black parishes were led by white ministers. Blacks who were free from the white gaze, even in church, were a threat to white domination. This caused a dilemma: the question was how to keep Blacks under white control and keep them separate at the same time. To decide how to handle the Negro problem, white bishops and laypeople met at the University of the South (Sewanee) in July 1883. The idea of forming a separate denomination for Blacks as the Methodists had done was rejected. The next proposal was to seek permission at the next General Convention to create special missionary districts in which all Blacks would be gathered regardless of geographical location.[69]

The Episcopal Church, especially in the South, found itself on the horns of a dilemma. For several decades after the Civil War, the stated desire was to bring more persons of African descent into the fold. In principle, the Church thought that a Black bishop could do much to evangelize people of his own race but despaired that "under existing church law individual dioceses elected bishops to supervise church work in their regions, which would mean that a Negro bishop would have jurisdiction over both Negro and white churches."[70] This was a concept that was abhorrent even to the more liberal northern dioceses. "Understandably, Blacks were desirous of the Black episcopate for the very reasons that the largely white Church would have barred their access."[71]

---

68. Addison, *The Episcopal Church in the United States, 1789–1931*, 199.

69. Hein and Shattuck, *The Episcopalians*, 101–2.

70. Lewis, *Yet With a Steady Beat*, 65.

71. Lewis, *Yet With a Steady Beat*, 66.

The Episcopal Church experienced a massive exodus of Blacks between 1865 and 1870, while the AME, AME Zion, and Baptist churches experienced astounding growth.[72] Here again we can see how racism warps thinking. The planter class could not imagine why Blacks would want to belong to churches or denominations where they were considered human and where they could exercise agency. As observed by Alexander Crummell, the founder of St. Luke's in Washington, DC,

> When freedom came to the emancipated class, by one common impulse they rushed from the chapels provided by their masters, deserted in multitudes the ministry of white preachers, in search of a ministry of their own race.[73]

Some Blacks remained in the Episcopal Church, and several congregations were founded. Sixty years before the Civil War, Blacks were ejected from St. George's Methodist Church in Philadelphia, and Richard Allen founded the African Methodist Episcopal denomination. In 1794 Absalom Jones, the first African American ordained priest in the Episcopal Church,[74] founded the African Episcopal Church of St. Thomas, the first Black congregation in the Episcopal Church that was to be fully governed by its Black members "forever." St. Thomas had to agree that it would not request to send clergy or deputies to the Convention or to be involved with the governing of the Episcopal Church. To have total control over their church, the diocesan requirements were accepted by St. Thomas. Later, in 1863, the restrictions were rescinded, and St. Thomas was admitted to the Diocese of Pennsylvania.[75]

In the years following the formation of St. Thomas, other Black congregations in the north were formed: St. Philip's, New York (1818); St. James First African Church, Baltimore (1827—although technically in the South); St. Luke's, New Haven, Connecticut (1844); The Church of the Crucifixion, Philadelphia (1844); St. Matthew's, Detroit (1851); St. Philip's, Newark, New Jersey (1856); St. Philip's, Buffalo, New York (1865); and Christ Church, Providence, Rhode Island (1888).[76] The Black

---

72. Michael Battle, *The Black Church in America: African American Christian Spirituality* (Malden, MA: Blackwell Publishing, 2006), 64.

73. Lewis, *Yet With a Steady Beat*, 42.

74. Bragg, *History of the Afro-American Group of the Episcopal Church*, 59–80.

75. Lewis, *Yet With A Steady Beat*, 29–30.

76. Bragg, *History of the Afro-American Group of the Episcopal Church*, 81–124.

Church, according to James Cone, was founded on the belief that slavery was not part of God's plan for Black people and that freedom in Christ meant emancipation in this world.[77] While this might have been true in the North, it was not a reality in the South, with the exception of St. James, Baltimore. In the South, there were no independent, self-governing Black churches and no Black clergy. Black congregants were still relegated to segregated conditions in white southern churches. While the Episcopal Church appealed to some Blacks, the Methodists and the African Methodists held greater appeal because of their egalitarian ways, and their numbers outstripped the Episcopal Church because it was continually identified with the enslaver and an overformalized liturgy. Interest on the part of the enslaved for the Episcopal Church was less than lukewarm.[78]

With the end of Civil War came Reconstruction. The federal government created the Freedman's Bureau to assist the newly freed enslaved. In a parallel move, the Episcopal Church created the Freedman's Commission in 1865. As should be expected, a white priest was named to lead the organization. Later the name was changed to the Commission of Home Missions to Colored People. The Commission's first report suggests that the Episcopal Church had done little for over two hundred years to assist Black people and had used religion as a tool to control Blacks and that the Episcopal Church "goes to great lengths to exculpate itself from any responsibility for the condition of blacks prior to their emancipation."[79] The church had deferred to its member slaveholders and had forsaken the gospel. The report continues: "[The church] seems to ignore this history and to seek instead the 'higher ground' of noblesse oblige."[80] Now, the Church would be saving the formerly enslaved from the negative influences of a society that had been turned upside down. Blacks who left the Church were seen as traitors who were at the mercy of, as Bishop Thomas Atkinson offered, "ignorant teachers of their own race who are leading them into the wildest excesses of delusion and fanaticism."[81]

While whites had done everything in their power to keep Blacks from learning how to read, the importance of reading and gaining an education

---

77. Lewis, *Yet With A Steady Beat*, 2.

78. Lewis, *Yet With a Steady Beat*, 35–38.

79. Lewis, *Yet With a Steady Beat*, 48.

80. Lewis, *Yet With a Steady Beat*, 48.

81. Bragg, *History of the Afro-American Group of the Episcopal Church*, 129.

was now seen as paramount to calling the strayed Blacks back into the fold so they could take their rightful subservient place in society. To that end, schools were established, one of the first being St. Augustine's Normal School and Collegiate Institution in Raleigh, North Carolina. Founded in 1867, its purpose was to prepare Black teachers, and later, its mission was expanded to prepare men for ordination, since it was thought that Blacks would more readily accept ministers of their own race and would not be drawn to Black ministers of other denominations.[82] While there were moves to ordain more Black men, and certainly there were eager candidates, only twenty Black men were ordained in the Episcopal Church between 1866 and 1877, and of that number, fourteen remained deacons; whites in the Episcopal Church were loath to admit Black men to Holy Orders. Deployment would only be along color lines, and there was a limited number of Black churches.[83]

Whites in and out of the Episcopal Church failed to accept their role in what they called the ignorant state of Blacks and blamed the victim for their lack of achievement. Church leaders mistakenly believed that by providing vocational and religious training, the problems faced by Blacks in a racist society and Church would be solved. Ignoring racism, it was simply a matter of making good citizens and Christians of Blacks, and they would be able to take their rightful and degraded place in a society that was neither prepared to accept them at all nor wanted to accept them as anything other than a servant class. There was no desire on the part of the Episcopal Church to work to eliminate racism in the broader society in which Blacks would live and work. As Harold Lewis writes, "the Church [was] apparently content to confer merely the outward and visible signs of improvement"[84] as opposed to working toward anything that looked like the reign of God on earth and to integrate fully Blacks into the life of the Church. The Church's failure to actually live into the gospel resulted in less-than-wished-for results in the attempt to win back Blacks who left the Church, and separate churches led by white ministers for the most part failed. Once ordinations of Black men did increase, the number of Black churches also rose, although Black leadership was still denied access to diocesan and general conventions.[85]

---

82. Lewis, *Yet With a Steady Beat*, 48–50.

83. Lewis, *Yet With a Steady Beat*, 51.

84. Lewis, *Yet With a Steady Beat*, 55–56.

85. Lewis, *Yet With a Steady Beat*, 57.

Failure to understand the role of white racism in the inability to either bring Blacks back to the fold or evangelize to new Blacks resulted in the elimination of the Freedman's Commission. At the General Convention in 1877 funds were withdrawn from the schools that had been established and were instead transferred to missionary work. Blacks who remained in the Episcopal Church did so because they saw the potential in the Church to be what God was calling it to be. Nonetheless, they knew it was the church of the plantocracy and that the religion they saw on the part of whites was an aberration of the gospel. Lewis writes:

> Black Episcopalians, then, could join and remain in the Episcopal Church because they saw it as their particular mission to help it make its practice conform to its catholic ideal . . . because they understood that "the Gospel carries implications which transcend the understanding of those who proclaim it."[86]

What to do with the poor Negro? In reality, religion is a means of control: what to think, how to think; what to pray, when to pray; when to stand, when to sit; what to sing, when to sing; what to believe and who to believe. The Episcopal Church wanted Black people for the numbers, but mostly, religion was used as a means to control the foreign population within white space—like a disease, a foreign body, that if let loose would contaminate the white people.

The Quest for Full Inclusion

Following emancipation, Blacks-only churches were not enough. Black Episcopalians wanted Black bishops; they wanted full representation in this Episcopal branch of the body of Christ. With white acquiescence, Blacks could form their own churches and escape the white gaze. With pressure and also the paternalistic bent of white church leadership, Black men could be ordained, but the subject of Black bishops remained a thornier issue. The bishop is the symbol of the Church's unity, and Black bishops would be a major stumbling block to that unity because Black and white unity in the church usually was and still is an oxymoron.

The ever-present proverbial question is what to do with the Black people. The Sewanee Compromise of 1883 to be proposed at the General

---

86. Lewis, *Yet With a Steady Beat*, 61.

Convention as a new canon was to further segregate Blacks into separate missionary districts within affected dioceses, which, of course, would be under the control of the white bishop. Disenfranchisement has been a weapon against Black people, and this canon would have ensured that no Black men would ever ascend to the position of bishop. Blacks have had to advocate for their own equality since they were first brought to this country, and in that vein, a group of Black men formed the Conference of Church Workers among Colored People (CCWACP), which was led by Alexander Crummell, rector of St. Luke's in Washington, DC. They decided to go to the Convention and protest the canon. Fortunately, the canon was rejected.[87]

Two main issues drove the southern bishops and probably the majority of bishops in the north. First, it was believed that the Church had no role in the cause of social equality. Second, there was the fear, as it is today with social enfranchisement, that having Blacks exercise their right to vote in church affairs would upset the balance of (white) power.[88] As Carlton Hayden writes:

> Most white Episcopalians were indifferent to the mission to Blacks. They frankly did not want Blacks in their churches, schools, seminaries, charitable institutions or legislative conventions. They felt that . . . the Episcopal Church was "so closely identified with the Anglo-Saxon character" that it was unsuitable for Blacks. . . . The "apathy" of most churchmen and the "failure" of the Church at large to support the Church's schools and churches among Blacks was the constant lament of everyone actively involved in the southern missionary work, whether Black or white, north or south.[89]

While the attempt to control Blacks by creating separate missionary districts failed, the CCWACP still had work to do. They had defeated the proposed Sewanee canon, and without something novel, it would be impossible to have any Black man elected to the position of bishop. The southern bishops proposed the use of archdeacons, who would have

---

87. Robert W. Prichard, *A History of the Episcopal Church: Complete through the 78th General Convention*, 3rd rev. ed. (New York: Morehouse Publishing, 2014), 228.

88. Lewis, *Yet With a Steady Beat*, 71.

89. J. Carlton Hayden, "Let My People Go: The Role of Blacks in the Episcopal Church," in Lewis, *Yet With a Steady Beat*, 71.

authority solely over colored work in the church. Black leadership recognized that if they ever were to have a bishop of their own race, they would have to retreat in their opposition to separate missionary districts within dioceses. While it might sound as if they were caving into white demands, they were not. In this proposal, the missionary districts would be under the control of Black and not white bishops. It was believed that with Black bishops, even within a segregated system, it would be possible to increase the number of Blacks in the church. What would be created would be a church-within-a-church with Black oversight.

In a sermon delivered by Rev. George Frazier Miller in 1903 to CCWACP at St. Luke's Church, New Haven, Frazier challenged the membership to take charge of their life within the white church, which might give them a voice at General Convention. A delegation was then sent to Washington, DC, to meet with a group of southern bishops to propose a canon that would create missionary districts with Black oversight. As a result of the meeting, the matter was first referred to the General Convention in 1904 and then in 1907. At the 1907 General Convention, the Memorial of the Church Workers among Colored People and the Joint Commission on Suffragan Bishops were established. This canon was also defeated in favor of a plan for suffragan bishops, which was presented at the 1910 General Convention. Southern bishops still fought for separate missionary districts at the 1916 General Convention and were still preaching racism. Bishop Montgomery Brown of Arkansas proposed that "a God-implanted race prejudice makes it impossible that Afro-Americans and Anglo-Americans should ever occupy the same footing in a dual racial church."[90] He, among others, continued to advocate for a separation of the races. The suffragan bishop plan was a way to maintain subservience and dependency on whites.

There were Blacks on both sides of the suffragan bishop issue; some believed it was the only way to have one of their own in authority, and others believed that to have a separate tract played into the hands of racists. The plan passed because it was paternalistic; it gave the appearance of Black control while permitting whites to maintain power they did not want to share with people they believed to be beneath them and incapable of leadership. This racist plan was the typical Anglican compromise

90. William Montgomery Brown, *The Crucial Race Question* (Little Rock: Arkansas Churchman's Publishing, 1907), 269–70.

because it would prevent, again, the church from formally dividing and would keep Blacks in a subservient position by denying the Black bishops a vote at General Convention.

Edward Thomas Demby, archdeacon for colored work in the Diocese of Tennessee, and Henry Beard Delany, archdeacon for colored work in the Diocese of North Carolina, were the first elected suffragan bishops for the dioceses of Arkansas and North Carolina in 1918. While they were revered by some Blacks as the hope for the future, they were denigrated by others because they were viewed as having little power and no voice in the church. Many thought of Demby and Delaney as bishops who would not threaten white bishops and not rock the boat. Two other churchmen— George Freeman Bragg, a candidate for the position to which Demby was elected, and Alexander Crummell, founder of the CCWACP to fight the Sewanee canon—were thought to be better candidates. Both were outspoken, and Bragg constantly challenged the Church and reminded it of its racist underpinnings.[91] Late in his episcopacy, Bishop Demby argued for the elimination of the missionary district plan, saying that there was a need for Black bishops who were suffragans but who worked as assistants to diocesan bishops. Eventually, his wish became reality; it was also the last time there was a suffragan bishop for colored work. In 1962 John Melville Burgess was elected suffragan bishop of Massachusetts with authority over Blacks as well as whites. He was later elected diocesan bishop in 1970, the first Black to hold that position in the Episcopal Church. Moreover, there would not be another Black priest elected to the episcopacy in the South until 1993, when Rev. Canon Antoine Lamont Campbell was elected suffragan bishop of Virginia.[92] Lest it be considered of less note, two Black men were elected bishop before Demby and Delaney. James Theodore Holly was consecrated in 1874 as missionary bishop of Haiti, and Samuel David Ferguson was consecrated as missionary bishop of Liberia in 1885. They were both succeeded by white bishops.

Controversy over how Blacks should figure in the Episcopal Church occurred during a frightening time in this country. The time of Jim Crow and the revival of the Ku Klux Klan marked a new militancy about race and an increase in white violence against Black people. Lynchings and racist laws were the terrorists' tools to keep Blacks in their place. The General

---

91. Lewis, *Yet With a Steady Beat*, 77–79.

92. Lewis, *Yet With a Steady Beat*, 81.

Convention adopted the first churchwide antilynching resolution in 1919.[93] Some viewed the Episcopal Church as becoming concerned with the lives of its Black siblings, yet this interest continued the paternalist direction in that upper-class white Episcopalians considered themselves the "natural protectors of African Americans."[94] While life for Blacks was fraught with danger, there were some advocates (e.g., in labor, civil rights, and Black northern civic organizations), which did not escape the notice of the Church. Again, not to lose control over Black people, the 1937 General Convention created the Joint Commission on Negro Work to improve how the Church related to Blacks. In 1940 the General Convention voted to bring forth a newer version of the 1883 Sewanee plan. While the bishops spoke of their desire for unity, their actions and those of most white Episcopalians showed otherwise. The plan was to create segregated missionary districts, and while there was pushback that identified the plan as racist, the bishops did not believe the segregated districts would denote inferiority.[95]

For the first time since his consecration in 1918, suffragan bishop Edward Demby addressed the Convention and spoke against the proposal. Representatives from the Commission on Negro Work, which was a biracial organization, also disapproved. There was dissension in the white ranks. The bishop of Pennsylvania, Francis Taitt, commented that Blacks in his diocese were as happy as contented cows and sought no change in the alleged unified church system. On the other hand, Bishop Middleton Barnwell of Georgia spoke to the inequity of segregation and pointed out that even when the General Convention met, Blacks and whites could not eat together or kneel together at the altar rail. He argued that until racism ended, Blacks would need a bishop of their own race from whom they could receive spiritual guidance. His appeal fell on deaf ears, with the other bishops arguing that Blacks received all the spiritual guidance they needed from white bishops.[96]

How to maintain the numbers of Black Episcopalians and also control them was the major concern for the white bishops. A separate racial district, while keeping the white church pure (i.e., white), would lessen white control over their African American flock. In 1942 there was a proposal

---

93. To this day, Congress has been unable (or unwilling) to pass antilynching legislation.

94. Gardiner H. Shattuck Jr., *Episcopalians and Race* (Lexington: University Press of Kentucky, 2000), 25.

95. Shattuck, *Episcopalians and Race*, 27.

96. Shattuck, *Episcopalians and Race*, 28.

to create a position, Executive Secretary for Negro Work. The white bishops were divided over whether this was a workable solution, with those against it being concerned about the loss of control over Blacks. The decision was made to approve the proposal primarily because the bishops could not agree either way, and on July 1, 1943, Bravid Harris, an archdeacon of the Colored Convocation in the diocese of Southern Virginia, was appointed to the position. Twelve white people were appointed to oversee and assist Harris in his new position, although his tenure was brief.[97] Again, "control" was the operative word.[98] Coinciding with Harris's appointment, the National Council adopted the "Guiding Principles Designed to Govern the Church's Negro Work," with four main criteria determining how the Church would deal with its Black members while also exposing the duplicity of the bishops and the Church.

- Fellowship is essential to Christian worship. Since there are no racial distinctions in the Mind of the Father, but "all are one in Christ Jesus," we dare not break our Christian fellowship by any attitude, act, or arrangement in the House of God which marks our Negro brethren as unequal or inferior.
- Fellowship is essential in Church Administration. Only through the privilege of exercising initiative and responsibility in Church affairs, through fair representation and voting power in all Church legislative assemblies, and the enjoyment of Christian hospitality with their white brethren will Negro churchmen be assured that their membership in the Episcopal Church is secure.
- High standards must be maintained to secure the best possible training for the Negro Ministry . . . [to] provide the same opportunities as those which are available for other racial groups.
- It is both the function and task of the Church to set the spiritual and moral goals for society, and to bear witness to their validity by achieving them in her own life. The Church is commanded to break through the encirclement of racial segregation in all matters which pertain to her program . . . and lead the way towards fulfillment of our Lord's desire that they all may be one.[99]

---

97. Harris was elected bishop of the missionary district of Liberia in 1945.

98. Shattuck, *Episcopalians and Race*, 34.

99. Heather A. Warren, *Theologians of a New World Order: Reinhold Niebuhr and the Christian Realists*, 1920–1948 (New York: Oxford University Press, 1997), 76–83.

The white bishops spoke out of both sides of their mouths. All of this took place during World War II, and as Gunnar Myrdal noted white Americans were failing to practice the color-blindness of the so-called American Creed.[100] The Church was also planning for a postwar world in which the goal was to build a better world for all peoples with the understanding that segregation contradicted basic Christian tenets. Still, the Church failed to live up to espoused beliefs and did not endorse ending segregation, and most white Episcopalians during this time continued to accept legally mandated segregation while hoping that the Church's "Negro work" would help struggling Black parishes and schools in the South. Appalling reports surfaced of the physical condition and poor curriculum at the Bishop Payne Divinity School in Petersburg, Virginia. There was talk of moving the school either to St. Augustine's College in Raleigh, North Carolina, or to Virginia Theological Seminary (VTS). Both proposals were dismissed with the admonition that the curriculum and physical condition should be improved or the school closed. Racism was the underlying consideration again; southern bishops did not want to send Black candidates to northern theological schools where they could not control what was being taught. A fundraising appeal for the seminary was resisted by some Black clergy who argued that asking for funds to restore a segregated facility was a grave mistake. Their proposal was ignored. Controversy continued over the future of the school, and some argued that Episcopalians should challenge segregation laws by permitting Blacks to be admitted to VTS and the School of Theology at the University of the South (Sewanee). Unfortunately, it was too little too late, and the seminary would soon close. No new students were admitted in 1947 or 1948. A vote was taken to close the school, and faculty and the one remaining student were transferred to other Episcopal seminaries.[101]

Prior to closing, the trustees of Bishop Payne and VTS met to discuss a possible merger of the two schools since VTS had been instrumental in Payne's founding in 1878 as a segregated institution. The decision was made that the financial assets of Payne would be shifted to VTS and would be set aside for the recruitment and education of African Americans at VTS. That fund remains to this day. While these discussions and transactions were taking place, John T. Walker, who would later become

100. Shattuck, *Episcopalians and Race*, 36.

101. Shattuck, *Episcopalians and Race*, 37–39.

the first African American elected bishop for the diocese of Washington, broke the color line when he was admitted to VTS in 1951. When Walker asked his diocesan bishop about attending seminary, Richard Emrich advised him to attend VTS because Walker would break the color line and would also experience racial hatred, from which he had been mostly shielded while growing up in Detroit. Walker reluctantly enrolled and later said that he felt as if he was "sitting in a movie called *Gone with the Wind.*"[102]

Not all white bishops were racist, and some even had the strength to speak out against segregation and the paternalistic attitudes of other bishops and the Episcopal Church at large. One of those enlightened bishops was the bishop coadjutor of Texas, John Hines, who would later be elected presiding bishop. He began to challenge systems that kept Blacks out of decision-making in national and diocesan level affairs. Segregation laws required that Blacks and whites attending diocesan and General Conventions eat in separate facilities. Bishops would have to visit separate gatherings to speak with everyone. In 1947 Hines challenged local and Church mores by demanding that all attendees eat together; however, he was rejected. He persisted, and by 1952 Blacks and whites ate together at local conventions. For the 1955 General Convention, Hines and diocesan bishop Clinton Quinn guaranteed that no one would experience discrimination or segregation for the session that would be held in Houston, Texas. Things slowly began to change, and Black Episcopalians were beginning to experience tepid equality in many dioceses. By 1951 the diocese of South Carolina was the only jurisdiction that still prohibited Blacks from full participation in the decision-making process.[103]

While change was slow, it was even slower at the venerable heart of the Episcopal Church in the South, the University of the South (Sewanee). All educational institutions come into being with a goal, an ideal, and the University of the South (Sewanee) was no different. Sewanee was the brainchild of Leonidas Polk—the bishop of Louisiana, a general during the Civil War, and major holder of the enslaved—who was concerned that few Episcopal clergy were trained to appreciate the "peculiar type of civilization" that was valued in the South. He believed that theological education could strengthen the institution of slavery, and to that end,

---

102. Shattuck, *Episcopalians and Race*, 39–40.

103. Shattuck, *Episcopalians and Race*, 43.

he encouraged nine other bishops in slave-holding states to support him in the creation of the school that would create an environment in which both future political and religious leaders could learn the tenets of "Anglo-Saxon Christianity." Polk believed that the enslaved would benefit from having well-informed and cultivated masters who would be critical in their transformation from being savages to becoming civilized.[104] Given this history, it should have been expected that when the Episcopal Church began to discuss desegregating its institutions, there would be pushback; however, the theology faculty at the University of the South protested because they believed that maintaining segregation was against Christian ethics. At the 1951 General Convention a resolution was introduced that stated that no Episcopal college or seminary should use race to deny admittance. Still, Sewanee resisted, and all active theology faculty resigned in protest. Finally, in 1953 Sewanee School of Theology was desegregated. The decision was not benign. It would be in the best interest of the Church to have Black priests who were from the South to be educated by teachers fully indoctrinated in the southern way of life to maintain control of the Black community.[105] Integration would always prove to be a thorny issue for Episcopalians.

Jesus Christ or Jim Crow?

"Do white church members in the South owe their primary allegiance to Jesus Christ or to Jim Crow?" Episcopal priest Das Kelley Barnett of Texas asked that question in 1957. It would seem that if "in the South" were removed, the question would be just as relevant today. In the early twentieth century, the country was moving forward, even if at a snail's pace, and the Church could ill afford to be left behind. The Church operated as a de facto segregated church in a segregated society. But when it became apparent that the Episcopal Church could no longer sit on the sidelines, it gradually began to consider wide-scale desegregation, particularly after the 1954 *Brown v. Board of Education* decision. The 1955 General Convention issued a strong statement urging Episcopalians to accept the 1954 ruling and stating that the church should welcome all people.[106]

---

104. Shattuck, *Episcopalians and Race*, 43.

105. Shattuck, *Episcopalians and Race*, 42–52.

106. Lewis, *Yet With a Steady Beat*, 148–49.

Some white parishes realized that their ministry was in a hurting and racist world; however, the question that was ever present was whether the
Episcopal Church was willing to be prophetic and pay the price, which
might mean the loss of members and the money that would go with them.
For too many Episcopalians, the Church was hypocritical in that it spoke
like Jesus but did not act like Jesus.[107]

White Episcopalians began to see their need to push the civil rights
agenda and put pressure on the House of Bishops to condemn racial
injustice. There was a need for an organization that would speak to the
Church as opposed to *for* the Church, and in 1958 the Episcopal Society
for Cultural and Racial Unity (ESCRU) was formed. It proclaimed that
"concepts of race, ethnicity, and social class had no place in the church."[108]
Members called out the Church as racist and caste-ridden. The goals
of ESCRU were the elimination of single-race parishes and the end of
race being used in admission to schools, camps, hospitals, and any other
Episcopal Church–affiliated institutions. The Church was being forced to
use its voice in the elimination of racism in society. By the middle of the
1960s, ESCRU membership had grown to over one thousand members.
For some, ESCRU had adopted a militant stance. Then, as today for many
people, "Civil disobedience . . . is just another name for lawlessness."[109]
For others in the Church, ESCRU was seen as an attack on white south-
erners who were just trying to maintain their way of life. One issue that
seems to be part of the perpetual fear on the part of some whites is interracial marriage; desegregation always seems to lead to discussion of interracial marriage and the so-called purity of the race. When ESCRU made
an official statement that interracial marriage is not contrary to the teachings of the Church, many believed it to be a grave miscalculation on the
part of the group that would distract from its real purpose, which was to
end all forms of segregation in the Episcopal Church and to foster interracial harmony.[110] For some irrational reason the ability to freely love and
marry whomever a person wishes did not fall under interracial harmony.

Integration is not without its own problems. Black parishes were
seen as a vestige of segregation in that they had served their purpose as

---

107. Shattuck, *Episcopalians and Race*, 89–100.

108. Shattuck, *Episcopalians and Race*, 101.

109. Shattuck, *Episcopalians and Race*, 103.

110. Shattuck, *Episcopalians and Race*, 105–7; Lewis, *Yet With a Steady Beat*, 150.

sanctuaries for its members. To integrate would involve a destruction of Black culture and tradition. Some Blacks, such as John Burgess, then archdeacon of Massachusetts, acknowledged that to move forward, Black parishes must be prepared to die.[111] To have a more inclusive fellowship in the Church, then, as now, Blacks were expected to integrate into white churches and to assimilate to that culture. The problem was that while Blacks were willing to make the sacrifice, often they were met with less-than-welcoming white attitudes. Further, within ESCRU itself, the founding members being white men, Blacks felt more and more marginalized, and in 1965 at ESCRU's meeting, a group of Black clergy presented a "Declaration of Concern," which asserted that Blacks continued to be marginalized and felt like aliens in their own church. In spite of this, Blacks continued to be loyal members despite their treatment, and they reminded the church of its catholicity. This was the same position that other proclamations, declarations, and statements of CCWACP had made. Black clergy believed that the bishops silently sanctioned the discriminatory treatment of Blacks, the race-based deployment of Black priests to only Black parishes, and called for an end to a restricted ministry in the Episcopal Church. Blacks challenged ESCRU to call out white supremacy and the continued paternalism of the Church.[112]

At the 1968 meeting ESCRU found itself divided into Black and white factions, with the possibility of dissolving and the Black Episcopalians questioning whether they could continue their membership. While this discussion was taking place, other Blacks had already formed the Union of Black Clergy and Laity (UBCL), believing it could better advocate for Blacks in the Church. Two years later, during the 1970 General Convention, ESCRU's vice president, Barbara C. Harris, announced that the group was disbanding. It was during the 1960s that all of this change was transpiring. The Black Power movement was in the air, so it should not have been surprising that the Union of Black Clergy and Laity (which later, in 1968, became the Union of Black Episcopalians) would come into being, intent on securing Black rights.[113] Indeed, similar groups were founded in other denominations.

111. John Burgess, "The Role of ESCRU in the Life of the Church," in Lewis, *Yet With a Steady Beat*, 152.

112. Lewis, *Yet With a Steady Beat*, 153.

113. Lewis, *Yet With a Steady Beat*, 154–55.

As has been documented, Blacks had always been relegated to ecclesial and societal purgatory. Church leadership had even taken steps to remove the Rev. Dr. Tollie Caution from his position as the secretary of the Division of Racial Minorities. This step was taken because the white leadership did not believe Dr. Caution could make the necessary changes the Church needed to conform to its new direction during the civil rights movement. This was a man who had given over twenty-five years of his life to this position, and he was summarily dismissed. This additional indignation was the catalyst for the formation of the UBCL/UBE.[114]

Whites-only organizations can exist, and people often look aside or keep silent; however, when there are Black-focused groups, which rarely discriminate against whites in membership, both whites and Blacks challenge them as being racist. Take, for example, the Black Lives Matter movement, a movement and not an organization, which some people believe to be racist when its sole focus is to have this country see Black life as valuable. UBCL was not welcomed by everyone because of its Black focus. Rev. Quintin Primo Jr. was elected the first president of UBE, which was comprised of three groups: The first was those who were committed to working within the system and were in the mold of Alexander Crummell. The second group had been part of ESCRU and had dreams of an integrated society. The third group were the young Turks, primarily those who were newly ordained and who drew energy from the Black Power and civil rights movements. They were committed to changing the Church, in the words of Malcolm X, "by any means necessary," and that was a threat to whiteness.[115]

Where Are We Now?

Between the 1960s and the late 1990s, racial change came slowly. In the Church's 1991 racial audit, it was reported that Black bishops were accorded less respect than their white counterparts. The Rt. Rev. Orris G. Walker Jr., the first Black diocesan bishop of Long Island, told his peers that while he was honored to have been elected bishop, he knew there were a number of parishes in his diocese that would not call him as rector. Having been elected to bishop, former president of UBCL

---

114. Lewis, *Yet With a Steady Beat*, 156–58.
115. Lewis, *Yet With a Steady Beat*, 159–60.

Quintin Primo stated, "The Church doesn't want us . . . in positions of authority." There were others who also spoke the truth of Blacks' experiences in the Episcopal Church, that they were not where the real power was found.[116]

While Blacks were having their struggle in all areas of the Church, women were fighting for the right to be ordained. Again, the Church moves slowly, and when the ordination of women did not pass the General Conventions of 1973 and 1976, those in favor took the matter into their own hands: In 1974 eleven women were irregularly ordained in Philadelphia. In 1975 in Washington, DC, four more women were irregularly ordained. These ordinations were a factor in the change in the canons to permit women's ordination as priests and bishops.[117]

Presiding Bishop John Allin continued with the progress that had been made by John Hines. The Union of Black Episcopalians was able to get him to establish an Office for Black Ministries and to appoint African Americans to his senior staff and African American bishops and clergy to various General Convention committees. Prior to 1974, only six African Americans were able to ascend to bishop, and only one, John Burgess, as diocesan. From 1974 through 1990, American dioceses elected ten African American men as bishop. Laypeople also played important roles. In 1970 Charles V. Willie served as the first African American vice president of the House of Deputies, and in 1976 Charles Lawrence was the first African American to be elected president of the House of Deputies.[118] In 2015 Michael B. Curry was elected and consecrated presiding bishop, the first African American to hold that position. In 2019 Deon Johnson was the first gay and partnered African American elected and consecrated bishop of the diocese of Missouri.

It would still take some time for Black women to break the stained glass ceiling. In 1977 Pauli Murray was the first African American woman to be ordained priest in the Episcopal Church. Barbara C. Harris was consecrated suffragan bishop of Massachusetts in 1989 and was the first woman bishop in the Anglican Communion, and Gayle Elizabeth Harris was elected in 2003 as suffragan bishop of Massachusetts. It would not be until 2016 that the Church would have its first African American woman

---

116. Lewis, *Yet With a Steady Beat*, 170–71.

117. Prichard, *A History of the Episcopal Church*, 330–31.

118. Prichard, *A History of the Episcopal Church*, 342–43.

as diocesan, Jennifer Baskerville Burrows, the diocese of Indianapolis. In her footsteps are the following women:

2018 Carlye J. Hughes, Diocese of Newark

2019 Phoebe A. Roaf, Diocese of West Tennessee

2019 Kimberly Lucas, Diocese of Colorado

2019 Shannon MacVean-Brown, Diocese of Vermont

2021 Paula Clark, Diocese of Chicago

2021 Ketlen A. Solak, Diocese of Pittsburgh

Yes, there has been progress, but if we accept the results of the 2021 Racial Justice Audit, much work needs to be done to ensure equality for all Black people in the Episcopal Church. Where do we go from here?

Reflection Questions

1. How and when did you learn the history of the Episcopal Church and race? Do you believe you received a complete history? Is there more you would like to know?

2. How does it make you feel knowing that vestries purchased enslaved Blacks and made them part of the property on the glebes?

3. Describe how you feel about the following statement: The Episcopal Church did not care enough about the enslaved, even those who were members of the Church, to split during the Civil War.

4. Have you read the 2021 Racial Justice Audit? What surprised (or didn't surprise) you?

5. What are you willing to do to ensure racial justice in the Episcopal Church?

6. How is your parish or ministry involved in racial justice?

7. If you are a person of color, have you faced racial prejudice or discrimination in the Episcopal Church? If yes, has your experience affected how you feel about the church?

8. If you are clergy, do you believe the ordination process is bias-free? If no, what has led you to that conclusion and what can be done to reduce or eliminate bias?

In Their Own Words

Female Clergy

I'm an African American woman in the Episcopal Church; I have navigated white space my entire life, my professional career. I wasn't formed in the Black Church as I came to my call working and living in a white community, so I never was in the Black Church pipeline. Once I became an adult and explored different faith traditions, I returned to what nurtured me in my youth. When I went back to the church, it was the predominantly white Episcopal Church. I've never been in the Black Episcopal Church; there wasn't one in the places I lived.

Female Clergy

I know more Black Episcopalians at [Black Baptist Churches]. My Black Episcopal friends make the 20-mile drive from the suburbs [to attend Black Baptist churches] because it's really important with their children being in white contexts, white schools during the week, that on a Sunday they have a community of other Black young people they can see. Back in the day we had Jack and Jill and the Blizzard Ski Club and other organizations that connected people from different churches. This is their way of coming together in community and providing community for their children.

Female Clergy

On Good Friday, I preached at an AME church. And when I preached, I felt good. I wasn't holding anything back. I asked myself, *Why can't I be this comfortable in the pulpit in my own church?* I remember the minister at the AME Church asked, "Do you feel homesick here?" No, I actually felt very good. But you know, it was before Easter, and they kept saying hallelujah. We're not supposed to say that. They were singing—the praise and worship. I feel like it warms me up for my preaching—like, we're supposed to be singing in public. I said I feel very Episcopalian in this place.

Male Clergy

On Sunday mornings, most of the time, I'm in a Black church, [and] I feel like I can say Black things without repercussion, which I do fairly

often. In my Sunday evening context, we have Sunday evening worship service with students; the vast majority of my students are students
of color. I don't feel inhibited in any way. I don't feel restricted talking
about Black issues; I don't feel restricted talking about racism, talking
about all the issues that plague our community and in the country. I
don't feel inhibited speaking as a Black man, and as a young Black man
in America, because a lot of my students are young Black men and Black
women and Black nonbinary folk in America, and they are struggling
with a lot of the same things.

Female Clergy

The congregation had been told I was coming. The senior warden, in his
announcement in each of the three services, cried and said there was no
place he'd rather be than at this church with [me]. Then it was time to
sign the letter of agreement, and he pulled out a letter of agreement that
was for $10,000 less than the job had been advertised. I said, "Well, this is
great. Thank you so much. Go to your next candidate, and I will happily
get on the plane and go back home, because it's clear to me you're not
serious." When the bishop signed off on a letter of agreement, he also
wrote a note on it, saying that he hoped that [I] would be grateful for this
opportunity. I wrote back and said to them that I am grateful always to
Almighty God, for the privilege of priesthood, but I was not going to be
grateful for the opportunity to be on this particular plantation for such a
time as I was earning my keep.

CHAPTER TWO

BLACK FIRST,
THEN CHRISTIAN

Moses was raised as Pharaoh's adopted grandson; Jochebed, his real mama, taught him of his heritage. Taught him of the God of the Hebrews. So even though Moses looked like an Egyptian; even though his hair was like an Egyptian; even though his clothes were like an Egyptian; even though he walked like an Egyptian; talked like an Egyptian; acted like an Egyptian, Moses was still a Hebrew.

—Rev. Carlton Byrd, "Quarantine Revival"

Y'all done sanitized the cross so much that you can't even smell the blood! Who throws a praise party at a public lynching?

—Rev. William H. Lamar IV, pastor,
Metropolitan AME Church, Washington, DC

White people. White people literally threw praise parties at public lynchings. A theology that resembles those perverse celebrations cannot save.

—Rev. Peter Jarrett-Schell, pastor,
Calvary Episcopal Church, Washington, DC

I know how to feel when I look to some in the church for help, only to have my faith questioned because I see in biblical texts a version of social justice that I find compelling. I put it all in the tomb that contains my dead hopes and dreams for what the church and country could be. I am left with only tears. . . . Christians, at their best, are the fools who dare believe in God's power to call dead things to life. That is the testimony of the Black church. It is not that we have good music (we do) or excellent preaching (we do). The testimony of the Black church is that in times of deep crisis we somehow become more than our collective ability. We become a source of hope that did not originate in ourselves.

—Rev. Esau McCaulley, Wheaton College

It was 2005; an Episcopal clergy colleague of mine was having coffee at St. George's Mall/Promenade in Cape Town, South Africa. He has been a priest for twenty years and has served various parishes in the United States. He realized that he felt relaxed in South Africa and began to ponder the reason for the feeling. Yes, he was enjoying a beautiful city that was African and also multiracial and multicultural. But it was more than that. Seventy-five percent of the people were people of color in the rainbow hues of South Africa. He became aware that he did not feel the white gaze or the pressure of code-switching to navigate the myriad of racially charged situations in the States. It was just him, and he belonged. Then he had an epiphany: "Damn, this is what it must be like for every white boy in America, the UK, every day of their life." There in South Africa he could be his authentic self for the first time in his life, at the age of forty-eight.[1]

Theologian J. Deotis Roberts writes,

> Blacks who copy the religion of the white mainstream because they have really arrived at a measure of success or make believe they have done so have no healing provisions built into their church life. . . . They are less emotional and are more consciously sophisticated in their worship than whites of the same denomination. . . . The minister is to be well educated and extremely polished, but he dare not extend morning worship for more than an hour. He must not introduce any Africanisms into his service—"gospels" and "spirituals" are out. Anthems are in. The preacher must not get carried away with his message. He must present in a clear, concise, logical and cohesive message. Not only must he steer clear of emotion in his manner of delivery; he must not belabor the cause of social justice in his message. It is my impression that this is not the proper climate for the visitation of the Spirit. What cost inauthentic existence?[2]

What is the cost of not being who God has created us to be? Who are we as Black Americans? Who are we as Black Christians? Who are we who are also Black Episcopalians? For Roberts, the question is one of "old

---

1. Personal conversation.

2. J. Deotis Roberts, *Liberation and Reconciliation: A Black Theology*, 2nd ed. (Louisville, KY: Westminster John Knox Press, 2005), 125.

wine and new wineskins" in which new wine must be produced in the area of race; however, we must ask whether the old wineskin—the Church—is able to contain the new wine of Black people determining their future and the ways they will worship in the Episcopal Church.

Can the Episcopal Church survive such a radical reshaping, reordering? If it cannot, what does it say for the future of the Church? Who will determine the shape of the new wineskins? If there is going to be change that radically alters how Blacks are viewed in and by the Church, Roberts offers that the actions taken must be on the "order of surgery rather than the application of salves to wounds with deep internal causes."[3] For there to be significant and lasting change, a new agenda for the Church must be written by Black Episcopalians, for as James Cone has written, only the oppressed can write the agenda for their liberation.[4] The heresy that is racism must be eliminated if the Church is to be true to its calling. Heresy, according to Cone, is the refusal to "speak the truth or live the truth in the light of the One who is the Truth."[5]

We Wear the Mask[6]

"Revival!" the sign proclaimed. It is not unusual to see churches beckoning people to revival services in the spring as if it is a rite of passage, but this sign piqued my interest. I was on the way home from an evening class I was taking at Virginia Theological Seminary, and I caught the sign out of the corner of my eye. At first it did not register, but then it did. It was in front of an Episcopal Church. From my experience, revivals and Episcopal churches were oxymorons. We don't *do* revivals, at least not in the manner of the Black Church. I had been to two other Episcopal revivals. When the late Rt. Rev. Barbara C. Harris was assisting bishop in the Episcopal Diocese of Washington, she introduced revivals to the diocese and brought in revivalists—preachers who can revive, bring or restore life to the church. I was familiar with one of the preachers, the Rev. Dr. James Forbes of Riverside Baptist Church in New York, and was introduced to the second, the Rev. Dr. Jeremiah Wright Jr. of Trinity United Church of

---

3. Roberts, *Liberation and Reconciliation*, 10.

4. James H. Cone, *The Cross and the Lynching Tree* (Maryknoll, NY: Orbis Books, 2011), 159.

5. James H. Cone, *God of the Oppressed*, rev. ed. (Maryknoll, NY: Orbis Books, 1997), 33.

6. Title of a poem by Paul Laurence Dunbar, in *The Complete Poems of Paul Laurence Dunbar* (New York: Dodd, Mead, 1913).

Christ in Chicago. The services were rocking and filled with the Holy Spirit. Bishop Barbara, with her Baptist-laced voice, set the tone. The Black folks were with it. The white folks, well, they looked uncomfortable. After all, this was in the Washington National Cathedral. A certain Episcopal decorum had to be maintained.

But, back to my encounter with the sign. I stopped the car, backed up, and read it—carefully. Three nights of preaching and music. Three whole nights? The revivalist was the same Rev. Dr. Jeremiah A. Wright Jr. I noted the dates and knew I would have to miss one night of class, but the sacrifice would be worth it to experience what an Episcopal revival would be. On the first night, I took my seat, not knowing what to expect. The Holy Ghost (yes, Ghost, not Spirit) showed up and showed out! The preaching was off the chain. The music brought tears to my eyes. The invited choirs were Baptist. The Episcopal Church's choir began the worship, and then the Baptists took over. There was call-and-response. There were shouts of "Preach it!" and "Alleluia." People were out of their seats, on their feet. When the first service ended, there was anticipation for the second night and then the third. The crowd size increased as the nights moved on. There were African Americans, Africans, and Afro Caribbeans. We were being revived.

Since I was looking for a church home, I decided to visit the following Sunday. It just might be the church I was looking for. I was shocked for a second time that Sunday morning when I realized the Holy Ghost had left the building and the Holy Spirit had yet to arrive. These same people who were up on their feet, clapping, talking back to the minister, and singing at the top of their lungs were flat. The frozen chosen had returned. After three nights of revival, that Sunday morning was sheer torture. Instead of being revived, I felt as if I had been given a tranquilizer.

I am not the only Black person asking how to fit authentically into a white denomination. In *Dear Church: A Love Letter from a Black Preacher to the Whitest Denomination in the U.S.*, pastor Lenny Duncan calls for a dismantling of white supremacy in the Lutheran Church. If we are honest, most everything about the Christian church in this country oozes whiteness, from church furnishings and art, the liturgies, to the lack of protests against the killing of Black people by the police. Duncan challenges Lutherans to confront the illusion that racism does not exist and acknowledges that most people in and out of the church are not actively racist but that they, like most white people, passively participate in "the spiritual and economic enslavement of every person of color."[7] He challenges his tradition to actively engage in eliminating racism in all its forms unless there is a desire for the Lutheran Church to "remain whitewashed tombs with merely the ghost of Christianity haunting them."[8]

Bryan Loritts is the lead pastor of Abundant Life Fellowship Church in Silicon Valley. In his book, *Insider/Outsider: My Journey as a Stranger in White Evangelicalism and My Hope for Us All*, he tells of being called "n——r" by evangelicals and how he has had to deal with the anger of white evangelicals when he has reminded them of their complicity in racism in and out of the church. He offers how he has felt when he was chided by other clergy when he preached on social justice, which for those clergy is part of the liberal agenda and allegedly not biblical. And yet, like Lenny Duncan, he is still called to remain in a denomination that does not have difficulty letting him know he is different, that he is not white.[9]

During the Great Awakening, Africans in America joined the Methodist Church in unprecedented numbers. It was the church of freedom; it was the church of abolition. In *I'm Black, I'm Christian, I'm Methodist*, nine African American Methodists share their stories, their experiences of being seen and not seen in the Methodist Church. They write of how the Methodist Church has experienced an exodus of young African Americans because the church has lost its centrality of cultural meaning for society.[10] These Black Methodists write of how the church is witnessing an increase in members who are mixing religious traditions in an attempt to find something that speaks to their needs as Blacks in America. The writers ask an important question for any denomination that hopes for evangelization and becoming what sociologist Elijah Anderson calls a "cosmopolitan canopy"[11]—a place, a sacred space, where race does not determine value. They ask whether Black people can justify being Christian and if the Methodist Church can offer hope—again.[12]

7. Lenny Duncan, *Dear Church: A Love Letter from a Black Preacher to the Whitest Denomination in the U.S.* (Minneapolis: Fortress Press, 2019), 16.

8. Duncan, *Dear Church*, 19.

9. Bryan Loritts, *Insider/Outsider: My Journey as a Stranger in White Evangelicalism and My Hope for Us All* (Grand Rapids, MI: Zondervan, 2018), 167, 96.

10. Rudy Rasmus, ed., *I'm Black, I'm Christian, I'm Methodist* (Nashville: Abingdon Press, 2020).

11. Elijah Anderson, *The Cosmopolitan Canopy: Race and Civility in Everyday Life* (New York: W.W. Norton, 2012).

12. Rasmus, *I'm Black, I'm Christian, I'm Methodist*, 5.

We are reminded as their reflections are read that "when a church does what it is supposed to do, as a church, it transforms not only the lives of its members, but the life of their culture as well."[13] Black Methodist congregations, like Black congregations in other denominations, assimilate into white, Eurocentric culture, which leads to the death of Black voices in the church while Blacks still occupy pews. And yet these Black Methodists stay (for now, as one has written), as do Duncan and Loritts in their denominations, in an attempt to make white worship space more egalitarian and reflective of the reign of God.

A church-within-a-church is an apt description of Black congregations or parishes in white denominations. Some, but not all, have been able to truly establish themselves as a bastion of Blackness in a sometimes hostile sea of whiteness. One church in the United Church of Christ, a white denomination, can serve as a template for how to live into Blackness while also being fully Christian. I have always loved the mantra of Trinity United Church of Christ in Chicago: "Unashamedly Black and Unapologetically Christian."[14] I hung onto every word, every syllable of the in-your-face sermons of its head pastor, the Rev. Dr. Jeremiah Wright. It was his forthrightness that caused problems for then–presidential candidate Barack Obama when the white media took one of Rev. Wright's sermons out of context. Any sermon by a Black pastor who critiques whiteness can find itself on the altar of "un-American" critiques. Those of us who were familiar with Wright and his sermons ignored the barbs of the media. Others tried to explain what he meant or tried to distance themselves from him. Trinity is a church, now under the pastorship of the Rev. Dr. Otis Moss III, that lives out the gospel of Jesus. This Black church in a white denomination is on the forefront of lifting up the least of these and living into its Blackness. There is no plantation theology, no otherworldly theology. Martin Luther King Jr. offered that many churches are so focused on heaven that they do no earthly good. That is not the case for Trinity: from the preaching style and music, from the Afrocentric dress, to its witness of calling out racism wherever it is found, to serving the least of these, this church lives into its mantra. Ancestral heritage comes before religious heritage—Black first, then Christian.

---

13. Bruce Birch and Larry Rasmussen, *The Bible and Ethics in the Christian Life* (Minneapolis: Augsburg Fortress, 1988).

14. "Our History," Trinity United Church of Christ, accessed July 31, 2021, *https://www.trinity chicago.org/the-history-of-trinity/*.

Our roots in the Black religious experience and tradition are deep, lasting and permanent. We are an African people, and remain "true to our native land," the mother continent, the cradle of civilization. God has superintended our pilgrimage through the days of slavery, the days of segregation, and the long night of racism. It is God who gives us the strength and courage to continuously address injustice as a people, and as a congregation. We constantly affirm our trust in God through cultural expression of a Black worship service and ministries which address the Black Community.[15]

In all of its Blackness, Trinity has no requirement that members be Black. All are welcome. As with other denominations, including the Episcopal Church, a seeker will become well-versed in the belief system. The United Church of Christ profession of faith has been adapted to meet the needs of Trinity's members and is the equivalent of the Nicene Creed:

We believe in God, the Eternal Spirit, who is made known to us in Jesus our brother, and to whose deeds we testify:

God calls the worlds into being, creates humankind in the divine image, and sets before us the ways of life and death.

God seeks in holy love to save all people from aimlessness and sin.

God judges all humanity and all nations by that will of righteousness declared through prophets and apostles.

In Jesus Christ, the man of Nazareth, our crucified and risen Lord, God has come to us and shared our common lot, conquering sin and death and reconciling the whole creation to its Creator.

God bestows upon us the Holy Spirit, creating and renewing the church of Jesus Christ, binding in covenant faithful people of all ages, tongues, and races.

God calls us into the church to accept the cost and joy of discipleship, to be servants in the service of the whole human family, to proclaim the gospel to all the world and resist the powers of evil, to share in Christ's baptism and eat at his table, to join him in his passion and victory.

---

15. Trinity United Church of Christ, "Our History."

God promises to all who trust in the gospel forgiveness of sins and fullness of grace, courage in the struggle for justice and peace, the presence of the Holy Spirit in trial and rejoicing, and eternal life in that kingdom which has no end.

Blessing and honor, glory and power be unto God. Amen.[16]

What might be the reception if the Nicene Creed was adapted for the Black experience in the Episcopal Church or if a new profession of faith was created?

There is something about lifting up Blackness. Black Lives Matter is not a threat, although it is often taken as one by whites who are wrapped in their privilege. Rather, it is an invitation to be more fully in relationship with one another. That is the beauty of the Black Church. At Trinity, lifting up Blackness is not an attempt to make whites uncomfortable. If whites are uncomfortable, it is because they have made whiteness the prize for all and they realize that it has all been folly. For those in the white world, the world that is "normal" or "natural," having tenets that are grounded in Blackness, that center Blackness, that put Black culture and Black life first, are seen as racist. Whiteness is fragile; it shatters, it breaks, and when it is not in the forefront, when it is not the focus, those who adhere to it can and often strike back. If the Black church in the Episcopal Church is going to survive, if it is going to grow and provide the support that is needed in a country that is bent on Black genocide, it will have to redefine itself. It will have to ask itself if it is the white church in blackface.

Authentically Black and Truly Catholic

Welcome to the Black Roman Catholic Church. Blackness before denomination; Blackness informs denomination. According to Fr. Jim Curran, who is white and the rector of Basilica of St. Mary of the Immaculate Conception in Norfolk, Virginia, "African American worship includes the fullness of the person so your whole being is caught up in the act of worship. It is so fulfilling. There are times I have to look at the ground to see if my feet are still planted on it. Because I feel like I'm levitating."[17] Of course, this is not the experience in all Black Roman

---

16. Trinity United Church of Christ, "What We Believe," accessed July 31, 2021, *https://www.trinitychicago.org/statement-of-faith/*.

17. The Virginia Pilot, "Inside the Only African American Basilica," July 30, 2014, video, 2:39, *https://www.youtube.com/watch?v=ajK63_p-gQ0*.

Catholic churches; however, African American worship has the ability to take over your entire body. It is bodily worship in which the Holy Spirit is visibly active and working. Rather than a worship experience, the goal is to experience worship.

In the 1984 pastoral letter "What We Have Seen and Heard," the Black bishops of the Roman Catholic Church began a movement that is still present today. They remembered Pope Paul VI's admonition to African bishops that they should give their particular gifts emanating from the African experience and culture to the entire Catholic Church.[18] The Black bishops took the words of the pope and extended them to all Black Catholics. They wrote:

> There is a richness in our Black experience that we must share with the entire people of God. . . . These are gifts that are part of an African past. For we have heard with Black ears and we have seen with Black eyes and we have understood with an African heart.[19]

The bishops laid claim to a distinctly Black way of worshiping, of being Roman Catholic, and of experiencing the world around them. They acknowledged that they were different from white Catholics, that their spirituality was different and distinct, much like Rev. Dr. Jeremiah Wright said about the Black Church: we are different, not deficient.[20] The bishops encouraged worship that was "in keeping with our African heritage [which contrasted with] much of western tradition."[21] Rather than separate themselves from the traditional Black Church, Black Catholics were to see themselves as inheritors of the Black Church in the tradition of seven historic Black denominations while holding to Roman Catholic theology and liturgy. This was transformational and brought to bear the best of Roman Catholicism and the Black Church

---

18. Michael J. Cressler, *Authentically Black and Truly Catholic: The Rise of Black Catholicism in the Great Migration* (New York: New York University Press, 2017), 1.

19. United States Conference of Catholic Bishops, "What We Have Seen and Heard: A Pastoral Letter on Evangelization from the Black Bishops of the United States," September 9, 1984, 4, *https://www.usccb.org/issues-and-action/cultural-diversity/african-american/resources/upload/what-we-have-seen-and-heard.pdf*.

20. MSU College of Osteopathic Medicine, "Rev. Dr. Jeremiah A. Wright Jr., Michigan State University Slavery to Freedom Lecture Series," February 28, 2002, video, 1:12:21, *https://www.you tube.com/watch?v=f8fIYcl5f3Y&t=1604s*.

21. United States Conference of Catholic Bishops, "What We Have Seen and Heard," 8.

tradition. With the support and encouragement of the Church, Black Catholics could live into who God made them to be, authentically Black and truly Catholic.[22]

Whiteousness

The hallmark of white moral injury is *egoethnocentrism*, the tendency to view oneself and one's racial–ethnic group as the moral and cultural center of all things. This is the cornerstone of white supremacy, the notion that white people (and the culture they produce) are the hegemonic ideal and thus represent the gold standard by which all other peoples and cultures should be adjudicated. White supremacy posits that because white people are the most beautiful and talented, they should be the faces that we see in magazines, on television, and in film; because they are the most intelligent, their books and theories (the "classics") should be the focal point of our educations; because they are the most authoritative, they should be the people in charge of . . . well, everything. White supremacy tells us that what is white is universally right and that any departure from the norm is a deficiency to be corrected.[23]

As he stood in front of the multiracial group at the Rooted In Jesus conference in January 2020, the Rev. Jemonde Taylor, rector of St. Ambrose Episcopal Church, a historically Black church founded in 1868 in Raleigh, North Carolina, led the group in a discussion of "Wrapped in Whiteousness: Worship, Liturgy, and Race." To this mostly white Episcopal audience, he spoke of "whiteousness," the combining of the words *white* and *righteousness*, coined by Mark Dukes, the iconographer of the Dancing Saints at St. Gregory of Nyssa in San Francisco. Taylor details how Western Christianity is the result of the suturing of Christianity and white supremacy and asserts that they must be unsutured. As he has researched, some Christian practices reinscribe racism rather than disrupt it.[24] There are words that seem simple and innocuous, such as *light* and *dark*. If Jesus is the light, then what are those who are dark skinned? Not

---

22. Tia Noelle Pratt, "Authentically Black, Truly Catholic," accessed August 14, 2021, *https:// www.commonwealmagazine.org/authentically-black-truly-catholic.*

23. Chanequa Walker-Barnes, *I Bring the Voices of My People: A Womanist Vision for Racial Reconciliation* (Grand Rapids, MI: Eerdmans, 2019), 150–51.

24. Episcopal Church Foundation, "Rooted in Jesus Conference," January 24, 2020, video, 1:18:24, *https://www.youtube.com/watch?v=3cLCtftMFL4.*

like Jesus? If the darkness is the opposite of God's purity and wisdom, what does that say about Black people, and how has that been used to denigrate and violate the sacredness of Black people?

To be American is to be white. To be white is to be normal. To be white is to be made in the image of God. To be Episcopalian is to be white, perhaps not physically white, but certainly liturgically and culturally white. We bring out Blackness in February for Black History Month and on special occasions. All other times are exceptions. Most of us assimilate to whiteness because whiteness is proper worship. Of course, no one will say that; rather, it is "the Episcopal way." Few will admit to that, but that is the American way: Whiteness does not have to be explained; it does not have to be justified. Whiteness just is. It is the brass ring that makes everything right with the world.

Assimilation

Though the word *assimilation* is common in our culture, we do well to take time to define the term.

> The main goal of assimilation in any nation is to change or convert cultures or peoples to become more like the nation they are joining. Culturally, this could include changing the way they dress or the language they speak.[25]

> The process whereby individuals or groups of differing ethnic heritage are absorbed into the dominant culture of a society. The process of assimilating involves taking on the traits of the dominant culture to such a degree that the assimilating group becomes socially indistinguishable from other members of the society. As such, assimilation is the most extreme form of acculturation. Although assimilation may be compelled through force or undertaken voluntarily, it is rare for a minority group to replace its previous cultural practices completely.[26]

---

25. Your Dictionary, s.v. "Assimilation," accessed August 1, 2021, *https://www.yourdictionary. com/assimilation#:~:text=1%20The%20cultural%20absorption%20of%20a%20minority%20group,of%20 nutritive%20elements%20by%20plants%2C%20as%20in%20photosynthesis.*

26. Britannica, s.v. "Assimilation," by Elizabeth Prine Pauls, accessed August 1, 2021, *https://www. britannica.com/topic/assimilation-society.*

The skin-lightening industry rakes in $20 billion a year. In the documentary *Dark Girls*, one of the several Black women who discuss the discrimination they face being dark skinned shares how as a girl she asked her mother to put bleach in her bath water so she could be lighter.[27] Assimilation has not worked. We have tried to fit in. We have bleached our skin and stayed out of the sun. We have "married white" so future generations would be lighter. We have turned our backs on our own kind to pass for white. We have internalized whiteness and self-hatred, we have relished all things white, and still we have not assimilated, we have not become white. We have not been permitted to become white because whiteness is an exclusive club, and those of us—most of us—of African descent have not been able to pass the test because the test was not created for us to pass. The church, the body of Christ—in the form of Western Christianity, the Episcopal Church—has also been in on this bait and switch. On this journey of embracing Blackness, of being (not becoming) Black and Episcopalian, the case is made that we need to embrace who God has created us to be and stop trying to contort ourselves to fit in and to become something we are not—white. In this journey toward self-acceptance, we tell the truth of how the Christian church has been a willing participant in the dehumanization of God's children of ebony grace; how the church has willingly participated in anti-Blackness, which is the inability to recognize, to see the humanity in people of African descent.[28] According to Kihana Miraya Ross,

> Anti-Blackness covers the fact that society's hatred of Blackness, and also its gratuitous violence against Black people, is complicated by its need for our existence. For example, for white people—again, better described as those who have been racialized white—the abject inhumanity of the Black reinforces their whiteness, their humanness, their power, and their privilege, whether they're aware of it or not. Black people are at once despised and also a useful counterpoint for others to measure their humanness against. In other words, while one may experience numerous compounding disadvantages, at least they're not Black.[29]

---

27. Image Entertainment, "Dark Girls," September 23, 2013, video, 1:11:50, *https://www.youtube.com/watch?v=J7GeGRulqYE*.

28. Kihana Miraya Ross, "Call It What It Is: Anti-Blackness," *New York Times*, June 4, 2020, *https://www.nytimes.com/2020/06/04/opinion/george-floyd-anti-Blackness.html*.

29. Ross, "Call It What It Is: Anti-Blackness."

I want to bring all of me. I want to see all of me in the church, the body of Christ. Is that too much to ask?

I was preparing to leave the church to go to the cemetery after a Burial Office (funeral) when a young Black woman approached me and introduced herself. She was Roman Catholic, and she said she expected the service to be familiar. There are similarities between the Episcopal and Roman Catholic liturgies, but she said there was something different. She could not put her finger on it at first, but then she knew what it was: a strange, exciting, new feeling of inclusion.

"When you went behind the table to celebrate communion," she offered, "it was the first time I saw myself in the service. Thank you." She was a lifelong Roman Catholic, and yet it took coming to an Episcopal Church to see herself fully included in the service because a Black woman presided over communion. How many Black people have yet to see themselves, to have their bodies represented in the body of Christ—their whole bodies, their whole selves? Why are there rules or beliefs that prohibit or limit the ability to bring one's whole self to the worship of God? And if it is possible to bring one's whole Black self to the church, what exactly does that look like, and what is required?

I have always resisted rules. Rules have always been limiting and stifling. I've always been the "Why?" child, constantly questioning, pushing, pulling apart, and sometimes putting back together. I was the child with the chemistry set that had explicit instructions about which chemicals not to mix, and I mixed them anyway, just to see what happened. Fortunately, the chemicals were not those found in adult laboratories, and usually the result was just a bit of smoke or effervescence that created a mess that I would clean up before either parent could smell my experimentation. To not have my "whys" answered was frustrating.

I first read Carter G. Woodson's *Miseducation of the Negro* in the 1970s. This quote has remained with me:

> If you can control a man's thinking you do not have to worry about his action. When you determine what a man shall think you do not have to concern yourself about what he will do. If you make a man feel that he is inferior, you do not have to compel him to accept an inferior status, for he will seek it himself. If you make a man think that he is justly an outcast, you do not have to order him to the back door. He will go without being told; and if

there is no back door, his very nature will demand one. His education makes it necessary.[30]

This quote by the founder of Negro History Week (now Black History Month) says so much about education, religion, law, our relationships in society and in and with the church—how we are programmed to see the world and each other.

I fell in love with Paulo Freire and *Pedagogy of the Oppressed* while in graduate school. It was there I learned that "our own technologically advanced society, which to our detriment acts to program the individual—especially the disadvantaged—to a rigid conformity; [thereby creating] a new underclass."[31] It was through the words of Freire that I came to understand the concept of *conscientização*, which "refers to learning to perceive social, political, and economic contradictions, and to take action against oppressive elements of reality."[32] It was through Freire and others that I learned how education is a tool that leads to the "great humanistic and historical task of the oppressed [to] liberate themselves and their oppressors"[33] from the clutches of dehumanization; that "dehumanization is not a given destiny, but the result of an unjust order that engenders violence in the oppressors, which in turn dehumanizes the oppressed." I have transferred *conscientização* over to church and religion. The fact that Black denominations and churches exist is prima facie evidence that an unjust order resides in the church.

There are times when I wish I had the time to fully investigate the Karl Marx misquote, "Religion is the opiate of the oppressed." For Marx, religion was used by the oppressors to make people feel better about the hell they were experiencing. In this country, slavery and racism would be that hell. Since religion is part of society and dependent on the material and economic realities of that society, religion reflects the inequalities present in society. For Marx, religion is "an illusion that provides reasons and excuses to keep society functioning just as it is . . . religion negates all that is dignified in a human being by rendering them servile and more amenable to accepting the status quo."[34] There are times when it seems that religion dulls the person to what

---

30. Carter Godwin Woodson, *The Miseducation of the Negro* (Las Vegas, NV: IAP Publishing, 2010), 15.

31. Paulo Freire, *Pedagogy of the Oppressed*, rev. ed. (New York: Continuum Publishing, 1997), 25.

32. Freire, *Pedagogy of the Oppressed*, 18.

33. Freire, *Pedagogy of the Oppressed*, 27.

34. Austin Cline, "Religion as Opium of the People: Karl Marx's View on Religion and Economics," Learn Religions, April 27, 2019, *https://www.learnreligions.com/religion-as-opium-of-the-people-250555*.

is needed in the world; dulls the person to Jesus's call for transformation; and in some instances, dulls the person to the oppression that is occurring. That we should just lean on the Lord, pray unceasingly, have faith that God will make a way; that all we have to do is ask and we shall receive.

Borrowing from James Cone in his discussion of the poor and liberation, "Without concrete signs of divine presence in the lives of the [oppressed], the gospel becomes simply an opiate; rather than liberating the powerless from humiliation and suffering, the gospel becomes a drug that helps them adjust to the world by looking for 'pie in the sky.'"[35]

The apostle Paul wrote, "There is no longer Jew or Gentile, there is no longer slave or free, there is no longer male and female; for all of you are one in Christ Jesus" (Gal. 3:28). The apostle John described his own vision, "After this I looked, and there was a great multitude that no one could count, from every nation, from all tribes and peoples and languages, standing before the throne and before the Lamb" (Rev. 7:9). Perhaps the wholeness we profess in Galatians and Revelation will come to pass in heaven, wherever heaven may be, but nothing on this side of the Jordan River has come close as it relates to the treatment of God's children of ebony grace. Still we struggle to be Black first, then Christian.

> What if we began showing people in tangible ways to proclaim that salvation doesn't require assimilation? I need you to hear me. I know you are a Caribbean church. What if you received God in your language? What if you received God in a way that celebrated your culture? What if you could speak to God in Creole and not French? What if you could come to God in Patois and not English? What if you could wear traditional garb and not a suit? What if you could come to God in ways that are germane to Jamaica; that are germane to Trinidad; in the ways that are germane to Cuba; in the ways that are germane to Haiti; and in that moment, you could see God and know God and experience God in a very unique and specific way because God is not opposed to descending down into your culture; [God] is not opposed to presenting [God's self] in a way that is unique to your experience! God is not against coming to you and letting you know that there is a decree over your life that overrides the decree of Satan and your salvation does not have to be wrapped up in white supremacy. Your salvation does not have to mirror that

---

35. Cone, *The Cross and the Lynching Tree*, 155.

of your colonizer. Your salvation does not have to mirror that of the European. Your worship does not have to sound European. Your shout does not have to sound European. Your dance does not have to look European. But you can come to God in all the Caribbean glory that you have. In all the Black American glory that you have. In all of the Afro-Latino glory that you have. What if we started to let people know that salvation does not require assimilation?[36]

The longer I live, the less I care about being an Episcopalian or even a Christian and the more I care about living the open table of Jesus, loving without judgment, and seeing what happens next.

The longer I live, the less I care about the "shoulds" the church has told me my whole life and the more I care about accepting the gift of who I and each of us is and is becoming.

The longer I live, the more I care about creating community where we all can come fully alive as artists and creators and the less I care about the ridiculous rules of who should be in and who should be out.

The longer I live, the more I care about gathering up the remnants and the less I care about preserving what has been.

And I hope, as I continue to live, that I will continue to care and not care more and more and more.[37]

Reflection Questions

1. Do you see or hear yourself and your culture reflected in the liturgy of your church? Have you thought about how others feel when their culture is not reflected?

2. Are you open to songs, prayers, and scriptural interpretations from other cultures in the liturgy? What might some of the obstacles be to inclusion?

3. Why are you a member of the Episcopal Church?

4. If someone asks, "What does the Episcopal Church believe?" what would you tell them?

---

36. Claudia Marion Allen, "For My People" (sermon, Fort Lauderdale Seventh Day Adventist Church, Fort Lauderdale, FL, February 20, 2021).

37. Rev. Mike Kinman, rector, All Saints Episcopal Church, Pasadena, CA, Facebook, February 5, 2021.

In Their Own Words

Female Clergy

When I started wearing locs, people asked if they could touch my hair. Oh, no, no. This is not a novelty.

Female Laity

Black people would come, and they would be very uncomfortable because it's not what they were accustomed to. They had worshiped in a white church. Again, we are historically Black, and we've invited all of God's blended family in, but we have to keep who we are as Black people and as a Black church because that's the only thing that got us through. Some stay; some leave and go to an all-white church. That's an option. People have choices.

Male Clergy

The [Episcopal] liturgy provides the framework and is incredibly flexible. So, for example, that litany we prayed (about the dreadlocks) came from the *African American Heritage Hymnal*. We pray that litany during Black History Month. The litany is not only about Black historical figures; it talks about beautiful Brown skin and locs and dreaded hair. Since there is so much flexibility, it allows [the church] to really live into what it means to be Anglican, Episcopal, or at least the American context. I think many times people say "Episcopal," and they think of a certain type of worship. But when we look around the world, my goodness, there's such diversity. When you look at Roman Catholic liturgy and its manifestations around the world, and Orthodox liturgy, they are incredibly diverse. We are able to tap into that, the catholicity of the church. That early principle that wherever the gospel is spread, it is spread in the vernacular, which not only is language, but customs and mores that follow.

Male Clergy

I sometimes supply and fill in at white congregations or Latino congregations in and around the city, and sometimes I think twice or a little bit more about how much I want to say about certain issues. But even with those congregations, even if they're white congregations, they won't chafe at me talking seriously about Black issues and racism. That's the great thing about being supply—I can say whatever I want. I don't really mind if I piss some people off, and sometimes the rectors really appreciate that. I'll say some stuff they would have more trouble saying, and then I leave. When I served the last two churches, they were predominately white, and I did have to hold back a little bit more, but there's less of that now.

Female Clergy

Question: Why do your Black members stay?

That's a good question, because I asked some of them to tell me how they came to the church and why they stayed. The answers varied. The music program for their children was one reason. Some people come from the Caribbean, and they were looking for a church near where they live. Some of them are gay or lesbian and wanted a welcoming environment that included social justice. One person spoke of worshiping here for almost a decade with hardly anyone speaking to them. In some regard, it's a mystery, because I don't think I would stay that long in a place if people weren't speaking to me. So it has to be something else. And that's an unknown factor. They obviously get some meaning from being here.

Male Clergy

Regarding making white people feel comfortable, I would advise, you cannot worry about that. Particularly if it's a Black space, historically Black or majority Black. You don't operate out of a posture of fear for the majority. The "normative gaze" is a phrase I learned in seminary. What is correct? The correct look—the white male gaze. To operate out of fear of disrupting the normative gaze—that is, whiteness—is problematic. So don't really worry about what Robin DiAngelo calls "white fragility," or white people getting upset, whiteness getting upset.

Female Clergy

There are Black churches, but a lot of clergy don't want to go to Black churches. That's what they've told me. They said they didn't come out of a Black Church. They haven't had an experience with the Black Church. They don't want to go into someplace where they have to struggle. They want to be where the resources are and where the people are. What would I say to them? I'd say, "Gird your loins." I would say know who and whose you are; that going into a white congregation does not require you to become white. They've called you because of the reality of who you are in all of the complexity of your being. Know what that complexity is, and know what it means. Know there may be a cost to pay for being yourself.

CHAPTER THREE

THE BLACK CHURCH

The Black Church, then, is the American fruit of an African root.

—Rev. Wyatt Tee Walker, *Somebody's Calling My Name*

African American spirituality is a spirituality that was born and shaped in the heat of oppression and suffering. . . . Blackness is a metaphor for suffering. To know Blackness is to be connected to the suffering, hope, and purpose of Black people.

—Dr. J. Alfred Smith, Allen Temple Baptist Church

All of us are bound to Mother Africa by invisible but tenacious bonds. . . . All of us have roots that go deep into the warm soil of Africa; so that no matter how long and traumatic our separation from our ancestral home has been, there are things we are often unable to articulate, but which we feel in our very bones, things which make us, who are different from others who have not suckled the breast of our mother, Africa.

—Bishop Desmond Tutu, Anglican archbishop, South Africa

Alfred Street Baptist Church in Alexandria, Virginia, is a Black Baptist Church. Everything about them cries out, "We are Black." Become a member, and regardless of your race, you will learn to clap on beats two and four. One of their major programs for the forty-and-under group is Come As You Are (CAYA). The topics Pastor Howard John Wesley discusses are those, in his words, "you won't hear from the pulpit." In one livestreamed and in-person segment, he was answering questions sent in by viewers, members, and nonmembers. One question piqued my interest. A young woman was conflicted about a Christian relative of hers who burned sage and used crystals as she prayed, invoking certain aspects of African spirituality or religion. The woman was concerned that a Christian should not be mixing traditions. Pastor Wesley answered her:

It is only in African American Christianity where we are taught to deny our ethnicity and our heritage. We think about Christianity and its connectivity—how enslavers used Christianity to make the enslaved docile. Christianity has always been able to blend/ incorporate elements of cultures which are not inherently antithetical to Christianity. There is a lot of African spirituality that is not antithetical to Christianity. It doesn't require denial or denouncement of Jesus Christ. It doesn't require us to toss the Bible to the side. Crystals, to rid one's prayer space of negative energy or using sage to cleanse—neither is antithetical to one's belief in Jesus.[1]

There is something special about the Black Church because at its heart it is African. It is more than the American Black Church and reaches back to the beginning of civilization in Africa. The Black Church reminds us that all people of African descent, wherever we are, are connected by a proud and vibrant past and history that was all but destroyed by the white Christian church and white supremacy. There are certain aspects of Black Christian worship that harken back to Africa and African traditional religion: the songs, the chants, the movements, the rhythms, the ancestors. Visit the Gullah Geechee Cultural Heritage Corridor, which extends from Wilmington, North Carolina, to Jacksonville, Florida. Here are African Americans who descended from enslaved people transported from West and Central Africa. When freedom came, most of the Africans and African Americans remained on the barrier sea islands and were isolated from the mainland. They speak a distinctly developed African American, English-based creole that contains elements of over eighty African dialects. They have retained more of their African linguistic, religious, and cultural heritage than any other African American community in this country because of their isolation from white culture and the white Christian church.[2] They know Jesus, and Jesus is not white.

Had it not been for the white Christian church and its complicity in the enslavement of Africans, the Black Church in this country, both invisible and visible, would not exist. Instead of buying or kidnapping Africans, if Europeans had instead stolen the concept of *Ubuntu* (I am

---

1. Howard John Wesley, CAYA (Come As You Are), Alfred Street Baptist Church, *https://www. alfredstreet.org*.

2. Gullah Geechee Cultural Heritage Corridor Commission, "Discovering the Legacy of African Cultures," accessed August 1, 2021, *https://gullahgeecheecorridor.org*.

because we are; and since we are, therefore I am),[3] the Black Church might not have developed. If white Christians had observed the Africans they thought were beneath them, they might have learned, as African tradition teaches, that no one exists apart from the community, the tribe. We would not have racism if white Christians had learned from the Africans that a person's freedom is tied to the destiny of the entire community. But they did not learn and have not learned; therefore, the Black Church exists. In both white society and the white Christian church individuality is prized over the needs of the community.[4] As Michael Battle offers, "African American spirituality is a unique model of human freedom because its very essence and nature are made in the social, political, and ontological struggle to be Black in America."[5] C. Fielding Stewart writes, "African American spirituality is the practice of freedom to create a viable Black spirituality and at the heart of Black spirituality is the concept of human transformation"[6] that both embraces and transcends white society. Black spirituality is about the transformative mission of Jesus.

The white church created a unique Christian form of white supremacy that still exists, and it is present in the Episcopal Church, divinely justified and undergirded by a specially crafted Christian theology.[7] This theology made it easy for white Christians to attend church at eleven o'clock on Sunday morning and then catch a train or walk in the church yard to participate in a lynching of a Black person without any fear of retribution from the God they said they worshiped. Historically, the white church has been a major presence in the denial of and resistance to Black equality; its members have defended segregation to the literal death of Black people and worked for the maintenance of white supremacy inside and out of the sanctuary.[8] White supremacy became the god whites worshiped after they heard sermons on loving their neighbor. Of course, their neighbor was not the Black person whose body parts had been cut off and passed around as souvenirs after a lynching. The white church interpreted the Bible to fit

---

3. Steven Biko, *I Write What I Like* (London: Heinemann, 1978), 24.

4. Battle, *The Black Church in America*, 11.

5. Battle, *The Black Church in America*, 35.

6. C. Fielding Stewart III, *Soul Survivors: An African American Spirituality* (Louisville, KY: Westminster John Knox Press, 1997), 23.

7. Jones, *White Too Long*, 33.

8. Jones, *White Too Long*, 33.

its white supremacist ideals. White Christians identified Africans with Cain, who killed his brother, Abel. Somehow, Eve gave birth to a "white" child and a "Black" child, and the Black child became a criminal, and that criminality has been visited upon Black people since they first stepped on these shores. Today, Black people still bear the mark of Cain and criminality as we see them killed by the police, incarcerated for crimes that whites do not even fear being incarcerated for, and shunned as inherently evil. The fears expressed by a Black mother at the beginning of the Great Migration in the *Savannah News* are with Black mothers (and fathers) today: "There is scarcely a Negro mother who does not live in dread and fear that her husband or son may come in unfriendly contact with some white person as to bring the lynchers . . . which may result in wiping out her whole family."[9] The Rev. Henry McNeal Turner, a bishop in the AME Church (1880–1915), wrote, "Until we are free from the menace of lynching . . . we are destined to be a devastated people. Lynching was evil not only for the victims but the environment as well. It damaged the entire culture; it poisoned the shallow well of good feeling between the races."[10] Lynching in its various forms is still a threat, as evidenced by the lack of an antilynching bill in this country. Black people are still being lynched.

To all of this, the Black Church called out the white church and white supremacy as a lie—a lie that has caused untold suffering to Blacks in this country. The dedicated Black followers of Jesus who formed the Black Church in all its iterations also knew that their understanding of Christianity, which was tied to a belief in racial equality, was more authentic than the Christianity practiced by whites.[11] James Henry Harris writes,

> All Black suffering relates back to evil—an evil grounded in American chattel slavery an evil that was grounded in white Christianity and white supremacy. . . . The Black Church has kept body and soul together for her children as racism and white supremacy become the milk of which white people drink. White supremacy makes white people struggle to be human because

---

9. Stewart Burns, *To the Mountain Top* (New York: HarperCollins, 2004), 32–33.

10. Martin Luther King Jr., *Stride Toward Freedom* (New York: Harper and Row, 1958), 160.

11. C. Eric Lincoln and Lawrence H. Mamiya, *The Black Church in the African American Experience* (Durham, NC: Duke University Press, 2005), 4.

there is a deterioration of the spirit, a spirit, according to Frantz
Fanon, white people don't seem to possess.[12]

In 2010 the Black Church was pronounced dead by Eddie Glaude
Jr.[13] The Black Church is not dead. The Covid-19 pandemic has shown
that the church is not the building; that the church is within each of us;
that when two or three are gathered in Jesus's name, the church shows up.
As long as there are Black people, there will be the Black Church because
it lives in the hearts of God's children of ebony grace. When Black Lives
Matter fights for the rights of Black people not to be murdered, the Black
Church is there. Black Lives Matter is the Black Church. The Black
Church is changing; the Black Church is alive and well; the Black Church
is not perfect. However, as Michael Battle writes,

> The African context of Christianity [is] the formation of self
> through communal being or relationality. [That] spiritual-
> ity means a rite of passage or a way of practicing a better life.
> The nature of the beliefs and practices of the Black Church can
> be summarized in the phrase *communal spirituality*. In other
> words, the essence of African American Christian spirituality is
> community.[14]

Because of the focus on community, the Black Church has given the world
the knowledge that whenever one person has been hurt, denied humanity,
or disadvantaged, "an incident of supreme importance has occurred."[15] Another aspect of African spirituality is the concept of *soulity*, which enables
Africans in America to transform negativity into something creative.[16]
We just have to look to the music created out of the soul-stealing, backbreaking evil of slavery. We look to the resilience of Black people to survive every attempt to destroy them. We look to the enslaved who did not
convert to Christianity; rather, they redeemed Christianity.

---

12. James Henry Harris, *Black Suffering: Silent Pain, Hidden Hope* (Minneapolis: Fortress Press, 2020), 30, 58.

13. Eddie Glaude Jr., "The Black Church Is Dead," HuffPost, April 26, 2010, *https://www.huffpost. com/entry/the-Black-church-is-dead_b_473815.*

14. Battle, *The Black Church in America*, xv.

15. Battle, *The Black Church in America*, 44.

16. Stewart, *Soul Survivors*, 23.

There Is No One Black Church

During the process of their becoming a single people, Yorubas, Akans, Ibos, Ango-
lans, and others on slave ships to America experienced a common horror: unearthly
moans and piercing shrieks, the smell of filth and the stench of death, all during the
violent rhythms and quiet coursings of ships at sea. As such, slave ships were the first
real incubators of slave unity across cultural lines, cruelly revealing irreducible links
from one ethnic group to the other, fostering resistance thousands of miles before the
shores of the new land appeared on the horizon—before there was mention of natural
rights in North America.

—Sterling Stuckey, *Slave Culture:*
Nationalist Theory and the Foundation of Black America

The Black Church is more than the seven recognized Black denominations.[17] It reaches beyond the buildings. The Black Church is a way of
being; it is a way of living. It is as varied as her children with their multitude of skin tones, beliefs, and practices. The Black Church did not begin
on the shores of North America; it traveled in the holds of the slave ships
that transported Black human beings throughout the Americas. Africans brought with them their religions, customs, songs, and myths as they
were forced to endure the Middle Passage and live in the lands that are
America. The Black Church is a reflection of every Black person throughout the world. Just as being Black is not monolithic, neither is the Black
Church. We are constantly defining and redefining it, molding it to meet
the needs of a people who have survived in spite of every single attempt to
exterminate us. The Black Church has only grown stronger in its various
forms and has not only survived but thrived because of the battles of her
people. One key aspect of the Black Church is the belief in the equality
of Black and white people (all people): human dignity is a basic right,
freedom is to be found in heaven and on earth, and love is central to all
human interactions.[18] The Black Church, when it does what it is called to
do, is God in action.

---

17. The seven historic Black denominations are: African Methodist Episcopal (AME), African
Methodist Episcopal Zion (AMEZ), The National Baptist Convention, USA (NBC), the National
Baptist Convention of America (NBCA), the Progressive National Baptist Convention (PNBC), the
Christian Methodist Episcopal Church (CME, formerly the Colored Methodist Episcopal Church),
and the Church in God in Christ (COGIC).

18. Henry Louis Gates, *The Black Church: This Is Our Story, This Is Our Song* (New York: Penguin
Press, 2021), 4.

While the Black Church is not dead, it, like the white Christian church, might appear anemic as we look at the accepted or normal way of being church, belonging to a denomination, and being in a building. Research tells us that membership is down in our houses of worship. In 1940 73 percent of adults belonged to a house of worship. As of 2020 those numbers were down to 47 percent across all faith traditions, not just those who profess Christianity.[19] According to Gallup data, an increasing number of Americans have no religious preference, and there is a decline in church membership among those who do express a religious preference. The number of "nones," those who do not identify with any religious tradition, has risen.[20] Ryan Burge, in his book *The Nones: Where They Came From, Who They Are, and Where They Are Going*, writes that secularization is the most likely answer for this reduction. Secularization is the theory that as nations become more educated and economic prosperity increases, religion becomes less important; the opiate that is religion is no longer needed. In the words of astrophysicist Neil deGrasse Tyson, as objective knowledge and science provide answers, the mystery and mystique of religion are no longer needed.[21] Burge points to the empty churches of Europe and cautions that it is foolhardy to believe that the lack of interest in church would not cross the Atlantic.[22]

As we look at the data, African Americans are more religious than the general population. However, as people are either leaving church or not becoming members, the Black Church is losing Black millennials. Why? Research conducted by D. Danyelle Thomas indicates that Black millennials cannot stomach a church that is laced with sexism, homophobia, and classism. They will not tolerate a church that does not feed them. Pie-in-the-sky theology does not hold their attention. If the church is not making a difference in society, not engaged in the transformative mission

19. Jeffrey M. Jones, "U.S. Church Membership Falls Below Majority for First Time," Gallup, March 29, 2021, *https://news.gallup.com/poll/341963/church-membership-falls-below-majority-first-time.aspx*.

20. Ryan Burge, "The Biggest Story in American Religion? The Unceasing Rise of the 'Nones'," Church Leaders, March 10, 2021, *https://churchleaders.com/news/391958-as-a-pastor-i-pray-my-flock-comes-back-as-a-religion-demographer-im-more-realistic.html*.

21. Masterclass, "Neil deGrasse Tyson Teaches Scientific Thinking and Communication," accessed August 2, 2021, *https://www.masterclass.com/classes/neil-degrasse-tyson-teaches-scientific-thinking-and-communication*. See also, Neil deGrasse Tyson on the difference between objective truth and personal truth, accessed August 14, 2021, *https://www.jacksonville.com/entertainment/2017-10-12/neil-degrasse-tyson-difference-between-objective-truth-and-personal-truth*.

22. Ryan Burge, *The Nones: Where They Came From, Who They Are, and Where They Are Going* (Minneapolis: Fortress Press, 2021).

of Jesus, they have other ways to become engaged in changing society. In terms of liturgy, Black millennials don't see themselves in what goes on in church on Sundays, nor do they hear themselves in the biblical texts. Rather than acknowledging racism and anti-Blackness as a systemic issue that poisons every institution in this country, too many pastors preach that racism is a matter of personal sin. Black millennials assert that they are too educated to overlook the fact that churches ignore injustice in the world and consign their LGBTQIA+ and non-Christian family and friends to hell. They want to be able to discuss their sexuality in church and not be shamed, and they are tired of seminars, for women in particular, that encourage them to "find their Boaz." Women do not want their sexuality policed; the purity culture has to go. Black millennials also see white supremacy in the church and want to do more than pray about it. They recognize that the church has power for change that is not being used.[23]

The Rev. Dr. Chanequa Walker-Barnes gave up church for Lent in 2017 and has never gone back. She echoes the reasons Black millennials are not in church, and she joins other ordained clergy, lay, seminary faculty, and students in their absence.[24] These are highly biblically literate people who love Jesus and are firm in their convictions that they cannot find Jesus in church. They find themselves in solidarity with Howard Thurman's deep discontent with American Christianity, as he described in *Jesus and the Disinherited*. Black millennials believe and want the church to live out what Jesus said in Matthew 25; they want the church to be in solidarity with the least of these. They want to worship God with their entire being; they want to bring their whole selves to the worship experience. They don't want to leave who they are in the narthex or foyer to worship. Since they can't find Jesus in church, they protest injustice, and they work with nonprofit organizations committed to changing the world. They want the church to take seriously the saving of God's creation through involvement in environmental justice; they want the church to transgress boundaries as did Jesus and engage in real interfaith conversations. Black millennials want an answer to the question inspired by Howard Thurman: "What word does Christianity have to offer for those who live with their backs against the wall of white supremacist, heterosexist, patriarchal,

---

23. D. Danyelle Thomas, "Exodus: Why Black Millennials Are Leaving the Church," *Unfit Christian* (blog), May 11, 2017, *https://www.unfitchristian.com/Black-millennials-church/*.

24. Chanequa Walker-Barnes, "Why I Gave Up Church," Collegeville Institute, October 12, 2017, *https://collegevilleinstitute.org/bearings/why-i-gave-up-church/*.

ableist capitalism?"[25] If the church cannot answer that question and work toward its resolution, the church has lost its power to inspire. Heaven can wait. White supremacy tarnishes our ability to be in right relationship with each other, and if we are not in right relationship with each other, we cannot be in right relationship with God. Further, research indicates that white churches continue to serve as spaces for the preservation and transmission of white supremacist attitudes, which can be a turnoff for many Black millennials.

If we assess all the reasons Black millennials are leaving church or don't choose to affiliate, we are left with the question: What has Jesus done for them? To some Christians, this question is an affront; however, young Black people are not afraid to ask tough questions, and they want answers. What has Jesus's life, crucifixion, and resurrection done for Black folk when they face racism and death simply because of the skin color God gave them? Why would a loving God allow that? Of course, there are the usual explanations in spite of what we face in society. We are taught about theodicy and that suffering strengthens us; that Jesus is in the suffering with us; that crying might endure for a night, but joy comes in the morning. For all too many Blacks, the tried and true explanations fall short, and they see no benefit in Christianity. Michelle Yaa relates that she spent her life questioning Christian doctrine. When she asked questions, the answers were not satisfactory. After consulting with her ancestors, she converted to Comfa, the Afro-American religion practiced in Guyana. Eboni Marshall-Turman, a Christian theologian, also provides a scathing critique of the Black Church and seriously asks what Black people get out of it. She acknowledges that the Black Church is in the world, that it serves the marginalized, that it provides that safe space where Black people can escape the white gaze and focus on their lives away from white hegemony. Still, she questions what Black people are getting in return for their dedication.[26] For Benedicte Songye Kalombo, Christianity is a distraction. She practices the traditional faiths of her native Congo. She wants to destigmatize religions that have fed her soul and believes Jesus hasn't saved Black people. She, like others who have turned to traditional African religions, believe that these practices are powerful, regardless of

---

25. Walker-Barnes, "Why I Gave Up Church."

26. David Love, "Black People Are the Most Religious People in America, But What Are They Getting Out Of It?," Atlanta Black Star, March 11, 2018, *https://atlantaBlackstar.com/2018/03/11/Black-people-religious-people-america-getting/*.

whether one believes in the supernatural. They believe that traditional religions can help knit together Black people across the diaspora and that American Christianity is a remnant of colonialism that continues to stigmatize these practices.[27]

The Black Church is not perfect, and those who question the efficacy of the Black Church ask where its voice is as racism destroys lives. For Black people leaving Christianity or the Black Church and for those who have never engaged, the Rev. Raphael Warnock, the senator from Georgia, writes, "The Black church is still 'an invisible institution,' rather than laying out a clear public-policy agenda rooted in a justice-centered theology."[28] In other words, the Black Church has been all too silent as Black bodies continue to be marginalized, fall victim to police violence, become fodder for the carceral system, and remain trapped in underresourced neighborhoods. How the Black Church is engaged in this world is more important than what happens after we are dead. For Warnock, the question is whether the mission of the Black Church is to save souls or transform the hell that all too many of God's Black people face every day. Part of the problem that might be leading people away from the church might be that the Black Church has yet to decide its purpose in today's world. To stem the loss of young Black people, the church must be, in Warnock's assessment, counterworldly and actively resist the dehumanizing effects of societal systems.[29] It must rediscover its purpose—why it came into being—and fight for the freedom of Black people.

Blacks are finding or returning to religions based on African traditions or spiritual practices. White Christian supremacy demonized anything African during the colonizing of African nations, and that legacy lives on today.[30] If we understand the wide swath of Black religion, then, as Josiah Ulysses Young writes, Black religion, which is anchored in slave religion, expresses itself in variations such as Vodun, Santeria, "Hoodoo," the Shrine of the Madonna, the Moorish Science Temple, the Black Jews, the Nation of Islam, and Kwanzaa, in addition to the Black

---

27. Yomi Adegoke, "'Jesus Hasn't Saved Us': Young Black Women Returning to Ancestral Religions," *Vice*, September 13, 2016, *https://www.vice.com/en/article/bjgxx4/jesus-hasnt-saved-us-young-Black-women-returning-ancestral-religions*.

28. Raphael G. Warnock, *The Divided Mind of the Black Church: Theology, Piety, and Public Witness* (New York: New York University Press, 2014), 146.

29. Warnock, *The Divided Mind of the Black Church*, 37.

30. Adegoke, "Jesus Hasn't Saved Us."

Church.[31] When discussing African American religion, it is much more than classifications of religions practiced by African Americans; rather, religion in this sense is a particular set of practices that are distinct from those practices invested in whiteness. These practices inculcate a cultural inheritance that mark the African American journey in this country, are a distinctive practice of freedom, and open up spaces that are closed to Blacks by white supremacy. These practices specifically reject the idolatry of white supremacy and offer ways for Blacks to imagine themselves free of the constraints of whiteness.[32] A religion steeped in a Eurocentric ethic is incapable of dealing with cultures that are not white, and not everything that has occurred in the journey of African Americans in this country can be addressed by Western or white Christianity. Ultimately, religion is concerned with how one sees oneself, how one comes to know and acknowledge one's significance in the world.[33] Even within the traditional Black Church, depending on how strictly religion is practiced, there is a non-Christian element that is resistant to European hermeneutics.[34] According to C. Eric Lincoln,

> Black religion derives, in the first instance, from the aspect of the Black experience that made it difficult to resolve the apparent incongruities between Christianity and Black slavery. It was not only a repudiation of the concept that slavery was acceptable to God, but has always been a critical medium through which the Black community has institutionalized its efforts to effect Black liberation. Inevitably this has meant a certain estrangement of the Black church from Christian "orthodoxy" as understood and practiced by the white church. Hence, the salient tradition of the Black religion has always been sufficiency of its own insight.[35]

---

31. Josiah Ulysses Young III, *A Pan-African Theology: Providence and the Legacies of the Ancestors* (Trenton, NJ: Africa World Press, 1992), 47.

32. Eddie S. Glaude Jr., *An Uncommon Faith: A Pragmatic Approach to the Study of African American Religion* (Athens: University of Georgia Press, 2014), 16–18.

33. Charles Long, *Significations: Signs, Symbols, and Images in the Interpretation of Religion* (Philadelphia: Fortress Press, 1986), 7.

34. Young, *A Pan-African Theology*, 108.

35. C. Eric Lincoln, "The American Muslim Mission in the Context of American Social History," in Earle H. Waugh, Baha Abu-Laban, and Regula Qureshi, eds., *The Muslim Community in North America* (Edmonton: The University of Alberta Press, 1983), 226.

For some, plantation theology—the theology that encourages Blacks to focus on heaven and not what is happening to their bodies here on earth—is still alive. Yet the hope that Black people hold must be grounded in the real-life situations that Black bodies face every day. The Black Church, across denominations and beliefs, must return to its grounding of being the center of Black cultural, social, economic, and political life. Religion, like African Americans and the Black Church, does not fit in neat little boxes, and we are free to explore what faith looks like in today's context.

Jesus or Christ?

In 1931 the Lutheran minister, theologian, and founder of the Confessing Church, Dietrich Bonhoeffer, arrived in New York from Germany. When Bonhoeffer came to Union Theological Seminary on a Sloane Fellowship, he became a student of the Harlem Renaissance and was involved with the Black Abyssinian Baptist Church, pastored by the Rev. Adam Clayton Powell Sr. This church was in the world; it modeled Jesus in the margins, providing employment and education programs as well as housing for those in the community and those arriving from the South during the Great Migration. This was in contrast to the white churches Bonhoeffer visited in which sermons were otherworldly and did not relate to what was happening in the world. Bonhoeffer wrote, "In New York [white ministers preach] about virtually everything; only one thing is not addressed, or is addressed so rarely that I have as yet been able to hear it, namely the gospel of Jesus Christ, the cross, sin, and forgiveness, death and life."[36] At Abyssinian, Bonhoeffer encountered a Black Jesus, while at the white churches, he found a white Christ who was not concerned with the plight of those who faced racism and suffering.[37] It was Bonhoeffer's interaction with the Black Church and Black theologians that compelled him to return to Germany in an effort to stop Adolf Hitler, which led to his execution. Bonhoeffer had adopted the premise that the minister's responsibility was more than saving souls; it was necessary to become involved in the elimination of social and systemic evils. Failure to do so would put the minister in collusion with the religion of the white Christ that Bonhoeffer

---

36. Reggie L. Williams, *Bonhoeffer's Black Jesus: Harlem Renaissance Theology and an Ethic of Resistance* (Waco, TX: Baylor University Press, 2014), 18.

37. Williams, *Bonhoeffer's Black Jesus,* 13–25.

found in white churches and that minimized the actual mission and ministry of Jesus[38]—what Bonhoeffer called "cheap grace"—and justified holding on to oppressive practices.[39]

In 1922 the Rev. Arnold Hamilton Maloney also discussed the difference between Black and white churches:

> The "white church" and the "colored church" are not the same thing. They represent two distinct psychological phenomena. In the former, the people congregate to render "service." . . . They pay God a call to offer their help in the difficult problem of *guiding the course of the world*. They make God their debtor. They bring Him down to them. To the latter, the church is a "meeting place." It is here that the talent for racial leadership is developed. It is here that the problems of home and of the community are threshed out. It is from this social meeting place that the souls of Negroes soar up "to meet their God in the skies."[40]

The African Root

In *The History and Heritage of African-American Churches: A Way Out of No Way*, L. H. Whelchel Jr. provides the foundation to consider Africa as the birthplace of the three Abrahamic religions, Judaism, Christianity, and Islam. Christianity is not of Europe, and counter to what many Christians are taught, Africans can be found throughout the Bible. Ethiopia is mentioned more than forty times in the Hebrew Bible. Egypt, an African nation, is mentioned over one hundred times. In the Hebrew Bible no European country is ever mentioned. Kush, the land of the Blacks, is where the two rivers of Eden are found.[41] In the book of Acts in the New Testament the Ethiopian eunuch discusses sacred text instruction with Philip and then is baptized. On the day of Pentecost people from Africa are present at the beginning of what would become the Christian church (Acts 2:9–11).

---

38. Kelly Brown Douglas, *Black Bodies and the Black Church: A Blues Slant* (New York: Palgrave MacMillan, 2012), 37.

39. Williams, *Bonhoeffer's Black Jesus*, 31.

40. Arnold Hamilton Maloney, "Whites Strive to Keep the Colored Race Divided," in Lewis, *Yet With A Steady Beat*, 10.

41. L. H. Whelchel Jr., *The History and Heritage of African-American Churches: A Way Out of No Way* (St. Paul: Paragon House, 2011), 7–8.

In the biblical text people were called "out of Egypt." The prophet Hosea says, "When Israel was a child, I loved him, and out of Egypt I called my son" (Hos. 11:1). In Psalm 68:31 we read, "Princes shall come out of Egypt; Ethiopia shall soon stretch out her hands unto God" (KJV). The infant Jesus was taken by his parents to Egypt when his life was threatened by Herod (Matt. 2:15). After being cast out of Pharoah's court, Moses finds himself in Elam and marries an African woman, Zipporah. The Queen of Sheba, who ruled over Ethiopia, visited King Solomon (1 Kings 10:1–13).

White Christianity has usurped the African influence, which has led to the belief that European Christianity is superior to African religious traditions and African Christianity. African Americans who are either leaving the church or who have never been churched are finding homes in African spiritual traditions and religions. If we are open, similarities exist between Christianity and traditional African religions, which both possess a concept of a benevolent Supreme Being, the dead being brought back to life, and justice for those who committed wrongs, and for those who are in right relationship with the Supreme Being, there is vindication.[42]

Euro-whiteness has erased Africa from intellectual history, and it shows in how Africa is dealt with in our educational system and the church. Kehinde Andrews reminds us that prior to Greek civilization, Egypt was the center of knowledge and well ahead in many areas, including science. All you have to do is look at the great pyramids, marvels of scientific achievement; we were not taught that "if you divide half of the perimeter of the Great Pyramid of Giza, built over 2,000 years (before the discovery of pi in the third century BCE) by its height, the number you come to is an approximation of pi."[43] Andrews continues that just as Europeans, in their white-revisionist history, removed the contributions of Muslims, the Greeks did the same to the Egyptians. We also learn, if we truly learn history, that early Egyptians were Black, of course—not American Black but Black nevertheless. Cheik Anta Diop in *The African Origin of Civilization* explains that "whenever the Egyptians use the word 'Black' (*khem*) it is to designate themselves or their country, for example, *Kemit*, land of the Blacks."[44] Egyptian civilization is traced to the Ethiopians who migrated north, and the reality of the history many of us were not

---

42. Whelchel, *The History and Heritage of African-American Churches*, 13.

43. Andrews, *The New Age of Empire*, 14–15.

44. Cheik Anta Diop, *The African Origin of Civilization: Myth or Reality?* (Chicago: Lawrence Hill Books, 1974), 4.

taught is that Africa is the home to science, math, and medicine before any of it reached Europe.[45]

African genius has found its way into hairstyles even though Black culture is viewed as deficient, defective, not the norm, and out of place in Eurocentric societies. As we read of Black children being suspended or expelled from school for their hairstyles, to understand the intricate braided patterns is to reach back to Mother Africa and her mathematical knowledge. In *Don't Touch My Hair*, Emma Dabiri writes of how the intricate braided patterns found in African hairstyles contain mathematical formulas.[46]

Every Episcopal seminarian is required to learn about the church fathers who have influenced the church, its rituals, and its beliefs. Some names might be familiar; however, was any emphasis placed on the African origin of some of these shakers and movers? It is important to do this so people are able to see themselves in the history of the church and to know that their people are part of the development of the church and that Christianity took root in Africa. There is Tertullian of Carthage, Justin Martyr, Cyprian, Origen, Tatian, Augustine, Athanasius, and others. Tertullian, the father of Western theology, opposed the mixing of Christianity and Greek philosophy. For him, Christianity did not need philosophy to explain its teachings and how it was to be in the world. Justin wanted to build a bridge between reason and faith, which should be familiar to most Episcopalians. He was influenced by Greek philosophy, which enabled others whose thinking was like Justin's to become Christian. Tatian fought against his teacher, Justin, and provided a difficult critique of Greek arrogance and culture. Considered by some theologians to be one of Africa's greatest investigators and interpreters of ancient texts, Origen is standard in seminary curricula. Augustine greatly influenced the doctrinal character of the Roman Catholic Church and was the bishop of Hippo. When heresies surfaced, these Africans found themselves on both sides of the issues and shaped the meaning of Christianity. Ancient Africa was the center of learning long before anything close could be found in Europe, and these African church leaders were highly regarded. They became some of the primary architects who have shaped the church as we know it today.[47]

---

45. Diop, *The African Origin of Civilization*, 168.

46. Emma Dabiri, *Don't Touch My Hair* (London: Allen Lane, 2019), 209.

47. Whelchel, *The History and Heritage of African-American Churches*, 13–26. See also Jerome Gay Jr., *The Whitewashing of Christianity: A Hidden Past, a Hurtful Present, and a Hopeful Future* (Chicago: 13th & Joan, 2021), 79–80.

These Africans were among the leaders who asked how the church could have leaders who lived a life of plenty and luxury while the people they serve lived in need and poverty. They were early voices against what we now call the prosperity gospel, and they challenged what they saw as the corruption and greed in the church.[48] In addition to the doctrines of the church, early Christian exegesis of the biblical texts is grounded in Africa. Methods for interpreting scripture can be attributed to Origen, Didymus the Blind, and Augustine.[49]

Christianity was not the only Abrahamic faith in Africa. Muslims who were African brought that faith with them to the Americas and faced the brutal system of chattel slavery. They brought with them ancestor veneration and divination and combined them with their version of Christianity. They synthesized their beliefs with those of Christianity to create a faith that sustained them. For them, God was Allah, and Jesus was Muhammad. While some Africans converted to Christianity, rather than it being a matter of belief, it was a means of survival, because conversion could mean freedom before the Christian church decided that conversion or baptism was not a means to freedom. Some African Christians converted to Islam because they believed Islam to be a version of Christianity.[50]

As Kelly Brown Douglas writes, Africans were not introduced to the Great High God who was known as Creator, Judge, and Redeemer[51] when they arrived on these shores. They brought God with them and created a Christianity that was totally at odds with what was practiced in the Americas. What we have come to know as Ethiopian Christianity and the Coptic Church can be traced all the way back to the apostles.[52] We read in the book of Acts of the beginning of conversion to Christianity with the apostle Philip's contact with the Ethiopian eunuch Judich, who was an official in the court of the Kandake of Kush or the Queen of Ethiopia (Acts 8:26–40) and who was baptized on a desert road at an oasis between Jerusalem and Gaza. The gospel of Jesus was not first preached in Europe,

---

48. Whelchel, *The History and Heritage of African-American Churches*, 30.

49. Thomas C. Oden, *How Africa Shaped the Christian Mind: Rediscovering the African Seedbed of Western Christianity* (Downers Grove, IL: InterVarsity Press, 2007), 45.

50. Gates, *The Black Church*, 22.

51. Kelly Brown Douglas, *Stand Your Ground: Black Bodies and the Justice of God* (New York: Orbis Books, 2015), 146–47. See also, Wilmore, *Black Religion and Black Radicalism*, 38.

52. Whelchel, *The History and Heritage of African-American Churches*, 39.

but through the Upper Nile Valley, by Judich. The first African Christian church was founded about 42 CE.[53]

This is more than a simple story in the Bible. With this connection between Judich and Philip, trade routes were opened to Christian traders. Fromentius, a Christian trader, traveled to the capital of Ethiopia in the fourth century. It was also during this time that Candace ascended the throne after the death of the king, and she summoned Fromentius, who introduced Christianity to the court, to be part of her administration. Later, Fromentius was appointed bishop of Ethiopia by Athanasius.[54] According to Gayraud Gilmore and others, Ethiopia became a major Christian nation shortly after the crucifixion of Jesus, almost two centuries before it became the state religion of Rome.[55]

In the debate over of who Jesus was and what Jesus was, Ethiopian Christians were fully on board with the Council of Nicea (325 CE) that held that Jesus was both fully God and fully human and that there was never a time when Jesus did not exist. In 451 Ethiopians opposed the Council of Chalcedon, which stated that God was human and divine, and that led to a split between the Roman Catholic Church and the Christians of Egypt and Ethiopia, the African wing of Christianity that became the Ethiopian Orthodox Church or the Coptic Church.[56] According to L. H. Whelchel Jr., "Christianity would not exist without the ancient churches of North Africa. . . . The history and heritage of Africa has been distorted, obscured, and falsified by modern Western scholarship—which is still seriously infected with notions of white supremacy."[57] Africans, the historical parents of Christianity, became "the children."[58] The influence of the African church waned, the history of Christianity was co-opted, and the focus of Christianity was shifted to Europe by European scholars.[59] The African roots were erased along with the memory of what was a more inclusive church.[60] As the European slave trade began to spread

---

53. Wilmore, *Black Religion and Black Radicalism*, 7.

54. Whelchel, *The History and Heritage of African-American Churches*, 37.

55. Wilmore, *Black Religion and Black Radicalism*, 8. See also Gay, *The Whitewashing of Christianity*, 106.

56. Whelchel, *The History and Heritage of African-American Churches*, 38.

57. Whelchel, *The History and Heritage of African-American Churches*, 45.

58. Whelchel, *The History and Heritage of African-American Churches*, 50.

59. Whelchel, *The History and Heritage of African-American Churches*, 50.

60. Whelchel, *The History and Heritage of African-American Churches*, 51.

its tentacles across the Atlantic, the influence of African Christianity on European Christianity was erased.[61]

Return to the Root

We need to recover our African roots and history. As we look at the Black Church, and in particular the Black Episcopal Church, in this country, repurposing the words of my brother Episcopalian the Rev. Dr. Michael Battle, there is a Christian spirituality that is African in nature that must be recovered and reclaimed.[62]

African spirituality traveled across the waters of the Atlantic, and it was the sacred cosmos that enabled Africans to withstand the disconnection, the humiliation, the violence of the enslavers. It was African spirituality that enabled the enslaved to survive under the brutality of the lash and the pain of the rape. African traditions survived slavery and also influenced how the Black Church assisted in determining a new identity for Africans in America.[63] It was the realization that African spirituality is concerned with the interrelatedness of all of life and not just one group of people or one species over the other. Holding onto African spirituality enabled the enslaved then and Africans throughout the diaspora now to live holistically, even if they do not realize it. It is an internalizing force that allows God's Black people to live with a view of life that permits them to believe in God, who is intimately connected to and dynamically involved in the world. According to Anthony Browder, it is not unusual to find "the Egyptian idea of nature as 'netcher' or 'neter,' also the synonym for God as corporeal manifestation ally of physical reality. A 'netcher' is not God, per se; it is instead an integral part of who God is." For the ancient Egyptians, the word spirit is translated *kha ba* which means "holy breath." This concept was later used by the Hebrews as *ruach* (Spirit). Then the Greeks adapted the word to mean *pneuma* (Spirit). In African cosmology, nature and spirit, creator and creation are viewed as a unified whole.[64] It was the freedom of the Great High God to be God, be the God who continually created and transformed reality, that gave the

---

61. Whelchel, *The History and Heritage of African-American Churches*, 51.

62. Battle, *The Black Church in America*, xv.

63. Battle, *The Black Church in America*, 27.

64. Anthony Browder, *Nile Valley Contributions to Civilization: Exploiting the Myths* (Washington, DC: The Institute of Karmic Guidance, 1992), 86.

Africans in the holds of the slave ships and those who endured under the lash hope. Using the words of Peter Gomes,

> Hope can seem a wimpy word, and it can be as flaccid as the typical Advent service, yet if we remember, as Paul reminds us, that genuine hope, a hope worth having, is forged upon the anvil of adversity, and that hope and suffering are related through the formation of character, then we will realize that hope is much more than mere optimism. Hope is the stuff that gets us through and beyond when the worst that can happen happens.[65]

This is the kind of hope that kept Africans alive as they struggled to make sense of oppression and dehumanization.[66] As they heard the Bible coming from the lips of their white enslavers, they were able to find the truth in those words, combine them with what they brought to these shores, and orally transmit a way to survive the horrors inflicted on them.[67] There has been an affinity between Christianity and African traditional religions for centuries, and that affinity crossed the Atlantic and informed the religion of the enslaved despite the ignorance and repression of the white Christian.[68] This affinity needs to be reclaimed today.

In *Ghost Ship: Institutional Racism and the Church of England*, Azariah D. A. France-Williams shares his experience as a priest in the Church of England. He writes that in trying to find himself in an English Christian story, he lost who he was. When you lose yourself, when you are uprooted, "you begin to wilt."[69] France-Williams, in sharing his experience, shines a light on what it is to be Black in this country and the Episcopal Church, that the act of loving oneself is an act of resistance to what is considered the Church and challenges any identity an African American forges for oneself.[70] Canon Eve Pitts, also of the Church of England, instituted an "Ancestors Arise Service," which received pushback from white clergy as not being "very Anglican" and because the dead, allegedly, must be left

---

65. Peter J. Gomes, "The Scandalous Gospel of Jesus: What's So Good about the Good News?," *Spirituality and Practice*, accessed August 2, 2021, *https://www.spiritualityandpractice.com/explorations/teachers/peter-j-gomes/quotes*.

66. Costen, *African American Christian Worship*, 23.

67. Costen, *African American Christian Worship*, 23.

68. Wilmore, *Black Religion and Black Radicalism*, 21.

69. France-Williams, *Ghost Ship*, 162.

70. France-Williams, *Ghost Ship*, 9–10.

alone, that there is to be no connection between the living and the dead. Ignoring white critique, Canon Pitts offered that the service created space to acknowledge and lift up African ancestors and permitted participants to embrace an African worldview. To be Anglican (or Episcopal) and to ignore that heritage, according to Pitts, is to dishonor the ancestors, who continue to give us strength to carry on in the face of oppression.[71]

The trading in human flesh by the British and others not only broke the backs of Africans, but it broke the rich religious systems that carried the Africans through the Middle Passage to the auction blocks and plantations of the Americas. The faith and spirit-filled traditions of the Akan, Ashanti, Dahomey, Ibo, and Yoruba people were partially destroyed by the slaveholding Christian economy. The Christianity experienced in the Americas was a degraded and degrading faith, and in the process, African culture and religion were all but destroyed. The traditional system of African kinship was also destroyed, and all forms of life were made precarious. The African family was destroyed. There was no legal marriage, and familiar relationships meant nothing to whites,[72] a destruction that has been used to pathologize Black people to this day.

Under Western Christianity, every attempt was made by whites to erase all memory of Africa; everything African was considered heathen, and no African history was considered worthy of remembering in this country of white so-called Christians. Robert P. Jones writes in *White Too Long: The Legacy of White Supremacy in American Christianity*, "Most white Christians continue to operate as if the theological world they have inherited and continue to sustain is somehow 'free of, uninformed, and unshaped by' the presence of African Americans. The power of this mythology can be seen in the fact that it persists even in the face of glaring historical facts to the contrary."[73] He writes that American Christianity has done everything it can to erase the fact that the beliefs and practices on which white Christians depend and believe are theirs are, in fact, dependent on an African influence they have tried so hard to deny and denigrate.[74] The Christianity practiced in American churches, regardless of denomination, unless there is a conscious effort to do otherwise, is

---

71. France-Williams, *Ghost Ship*, 45.

72. Frazier, *The Negro Church in America*, 13.

73. Jones, *White Too Long*, 22–23.

74. Jones, *White Too Long*, 22.

a Christianity that "white Christians literally built—architecturally, culturally, and theologically—white supremacy into an American Christianity that held an *a priori* commitment to slavery and segregation,"[75] which "still transmits and reinforces white supremacist attitudes"[76] in its pews and to future generations. Jones further asserts that because of the racism that is inherent in American Christianity, adding "Christian" to the average white person's identity "moves him or her toward more, not less, affinity with white supremacy."[77] White Christianity also negated identity as Christians in that race became more important than baptism.[78] With this background, American Christianity has at its foundation a deep white supremacist racial identity. It is not difficult to understand that to be white is to be American and Christian. For everyone else, their humanity and faith tradition is subject to speculation.[79]

Africans in America

The African Church in its various forms, the forerunner of the Black Church in the Americas, did not disappear regardless of the efforts of white so-called Christians. White Christianity could not totally erase the indigenous religions and practices and African Christianity that survived on these shores. Africans in America would still worship in a way that lifted up their humanity. Their syncretized religion would prove to be the focus of resistance.[80] Although ancestor veneration, dancing, drumming, shouting, and being possessed by deities were seen as pagan by white Christians, Africans in America would steal away to the forests, bogs, and hush harbors to practice their beliefs. They would also take those aspects of Christianity that had not been corrupted by whites—for example, that Jesus died for our sins or that Jesus became incarnate and inaugurated God's reign on earth—and incorporate them into what became a unique and blended form of worship. As decades and generations came and went, some practices were forgotten and not passed on, and as some Africans

---

75. Jones, *White Too Long*, 187.

76. Jones, *White Too Long*, 186.

77. Jones, *White Too Long*, 187.

78. Battle, *The Black Church in America*, 29.

79. Battle, *The Black Church in America*, 47.

80. Wyatt T. Walker, *Somebody's Calling My Name: Black Sacred Music and Social Change* (Valley Forge, PA: Judson Press, 1979), 45.

converted to American Christianity, it was still theirs to make even under the threat of physical violence or death by the enslavers.[81] Black Christianity has not been a shrinking violet. We must never forget the role of Black faith in the slave rebellions of Nat Turner, Gabriel Prosser, and Denmark Vesey.[82] The Christianity of the white enslaver was Africanized.[83] In addition to the Black Church being made necessary because of white racism, the Black Church also came into being to redefine African identity from savage, brutish, unintelligent, criminal, lascivious, and other negative terms that were created by white Americans and white Christians in their attempt to justify their racism.[84] Africanized Christianity is being resurrected by those who are willing to challenge ancient doctrines and beliefs.

Music was very important in African spirituality, and it is critical that the meaning of the spirituals be understood in terms of their religious and social contexts. These are more than what one African Methodist Episcopal bishop called "corn field ditties, songs of fist and hell worshippers." For this bishop and others who were averse to slave songs, there was a desire to drive out "heathenish mode(s) of worship" because they were believed to lack intelligence and refinement.[85] These songs were communal songs that were developed extemporaneously and given to the particular situation in which the enslaved found themselves. They were heartfelt. Many were formed out of traditional African tunes that had survived the brutality of slavery.[86] If we listen today, many of the songs are otherworldly because there was nothing to look forward to in this world. Wyatt Tee Walker writes that the spirituals of the enslaved were the umbrella "for the many cries and expressions of the human spirit in bondage. *In bondage!*"[87] Walker wants it known and remembered that spirituals were created by a people who were held in bondage, whose freedom was controlled by others, who were not seen as being human. Spirituals were the result of

---

81. Whelchel, *The History and Heritage of African-American Churches*, 82–83.

82. Gates, *The Black Church*, xvii–xviii.

83. Lerome Bennett Jr., *Before the Mayflower: A History of the Negro in America, 1619–1964*, rev. ed. (Baltimore: Penguin Books, 1966), 189.

84. Battle, *The Black Church in America*, 28.

85. Frazier, *The Negro Church in America*, 37.

86. Albert J. Raboteau, *Slave Religion: The "Invisible Institution" in the Antebellum South* (New York: Oxford University Press, 2004), 243.

87. Walker, *Somebody's Calling My Name*, 43.

the genocide of the slave trade combined with the brutality and terror of slavery. While the destruction of African traditions and customs was the goal of the enslavers, they could not destroy the oral tradition of the Africans' heritage, and while instruments such as the drums were forbidden, the voice remained. The music, in the words of the rapper Common from the song "Glory" in the movie *Selma*, "The music is the cuts that we bleed through." The music was the expression of the hell that was being experienced and of freedom and peace.[88] The essence of antebellum Black religion through music was a unique emphasis on the somebodiness of the enslaved as opposed to chattel property of the enslaver.[89]

It was during the Great Awakening that the Black Church came out of the hush harbors and Blacks began to form an identity as Christians for themselves. For many that faith led them to free themselves from white oppression through open rebellion.[90] In what would come to be known as the Stono Rebellion, on September 9, 1739,[91] Africans rose up and killed about twenty-five whites in Charleston, South Carolina. Whites who would use violence to overthrow their own English oppressor in 1776 could not see that same drive in Africans who had been denied liberty. Rebellion, backed by biblical apocalyptic readings, provided Blacks with the spiritual strength to resist oppression with sometimes tragic results. Death was not an obstacle to seeking freedom.[92] As would be the case throughout the history of Blacks in America, Black rebellion was met with increasingly frequent white violence to keep Blacks under control, and churches that catered to Blacks were closed because they were viewed as places that fomented violence against whites.[93]

Wanting their own sacred space, Blacks began to form their own churches. The Silver Bluff Baptist Church in Beech Island, South Carolina, was the first formal Black church in this country. Founded between 1773 and 1775, it is the womb out of which Baptist Mission and schools, not only in this country but also around the African diaspora were founded.[94] As more and more Africans in America took hold and shaped

---

88. Walker, *Somebody's Calling My Name*, 45.

89. James H. Cone, *The Spirituals and the Blues* (Maryknoll, NY: Orbis Books, 1972), 17.

90. Gates, *The Black Church*, 41.

91. Gates, *The Black Church*, 79.

92. Wilmore, *Black Religion and Black Radicalism*, 97.

93. Whelchel, *The History and Heritage of African-American Churches*, 93.

94. Whelchel, *The History and Heritage of African-American Churches*, 98–99.

their brand of Christianity, the independent Black preacher was born. As a result, more Black churches were founded and included "African" in their names. The First African Baptist Church of Augusta, Georgia, later changed its name to Springfield Baptist Church and gave birth in 1867 to Morehouse College.[95] Education would prove to be important in Africans' quest for freedom, and the Black Church would be the site of formal and informal schools. The clamp down on education for Blacks that was fomented with the Stono Rebellion was unlocked by the Black Church.[96]

The first Black denomination and the first Black Episcopal Church were both the result of white Christian racism. Both Richard Allen, the founder of the African Methodist Episcopal Church, and Absalom Jones, the first African American ordained priest in the Episcopal Church, were members of St. George's Methodist Church in Philadelphia. Both had worked tirelessly to increase membership of the interracial church. As experience and statistics bear out, there is a tipping point when the presence of too many Blacks upsets white comfort. Plus, there was the issue of Black leadership. Blacks are not supposed to be in positions of leadership, not even when that leadership was of other Blacks. The tension at St. George's resulted in Allen suggesting that Blacks create a worship space specifically for them. Since they would not be under the white gaze, his request was denied. The Black members also requested their own study group, which was similarly turned down. Finally, the last straw occurred on a Sunday in November 1787, when Allen, Jones, and other Black members were kneeling in prayer and were disturbed by white trustees who pulled them up and told them they could not kneel at the altar. Jones told them to wait until their prayer was over, but the trustees refused and forced them to end their prayer. Jones and Allen led the Black members out of St. George's, never to return.[97]

While Allen preferred the Methodist Church, most of the Black members who left St. George's preferred the Episcopal Church, which seemed to be more amenable to Black people at the time. They were also reluctant to begin a new denomination. Richard Allen could have become the first African American ordained in this country if he had accepted the offer from the Episcopal Church. Allen refused, believing

---

95. Gates, *The Black Church*, 43, 84.

96. Gates, *The Black Church*, 68.

97. Gates, *The Black Church*, 47.

the Methodist way was more suitable for Black people, and the Episcopal Church ordained Absalom Jones after several twists and turns.[98]

Before moving on to found the African Methodist Episcopal Church and Jones founding The African Episcopal Church of St. Thomas, Jones and Allen led the Free African Society (FAS). While not technically a religious institution, the FAS contained various forms of the Black Church in its positive effects on the lives of Africans in America. The Society, organized on April 12, 1787, was a mutual aid society, and during the yellow fever epidemic of 1793, the FAS provided nursing, transport, and burial services to the city of Philadelphia, at the time the US capital and the largest city in the country. All federal government officials left the city, as did others who could escape, leaving behind the poor, the sick, and the Black people. In what can only be called medical apartheid, Blacks of Philadelphia were asked to assist because it was believed they were immune to the disease. After prayer and consultation, Jones and Allen agreed to assist.[99] The Black Church in its various forms has always offered services, religious or otherwise, regardless of color.

After the Civil War, Black churches and their preachers led the way for improved conditions for both previously free Blacks and those who were emancipated. It was not unusual for Black preachers to risk violence and death to fight against or work with governmental officials. Of course, this ability upset whites because it further destroyed the myth of white supremacy that Blacks were incapable of being anything other than beasts of burden and brood mares. For the Black Church, preachers played an outsized role in the political scene during Reconstruction. Looking at the life of Jesus, for Blacks and their ministers, "it was impossible to separate religion from politics."[100] During Reconstruction, more than one hundred Black ministers served in political positions, from mayor, to police chief, to senator.[101] One such minister was Rev. Henry McNeal Turner, who preached a message of liberation that upset whites. Free-born in 1834, Turner was the son of African royalty, and he was bold enough to be the first known clergy person to preach that God was Black. He said:

---

98. Whelchel, *The History and Heritage of African-American Churches*, 110.

99. Absalom Jones and Richard Allen, "A Narrative of the Proceedings of the Black People during the Late Awful Calamity in Philadelphia, in the Year 1793," accessed August 2, 2021, *https://nrs. harvard.edu/urn-3:HMS.COUNT:1115398.*

100. Gates, *The Black Church*, 93.

101. Whelchel, *The History and Heritage of African-American Churches*, 138.

We have as much right biblically and otherwise to believe that God is a Negro, as you buckra or white people have to believe that God is a fine looking, symmetrical and ornamented white man. For the bulk of you and all the fool Negroes of this country who believe that God is a white-skinned, blue-eyed, straight-haired, projected nose, compressed lipped, finely robed white gentleman sitting upon a throne somewhere in heaven. Every race of people since time began who have attempted to describe their God by words or by painting or carving or by any form or figure have conveyed the idea that the God who made them and shaped their destinies was symbolized in themselves, and why should not the Negro believe that he resembles God as much as other people? This is one of the reasons we favor African emigration, or Negro naturalization, wherever we can find a domain, for, as long as we remain among the whites the Negro will believe that the devil is Black and that he [the Negro] favors the devil and that God is white and he [the Negro] bears no resemblance to him, and the effect of such sentiment is contemptuous and degrading and one half of the Negroes will be trying to get white and the other half will spend their days in trying to be white men's scullions in order to please the whites."[102]

This minister, this bishop of the AME Church, was no turn-the-other-cheek Christian. He believed that Black religion was a protest movement against white racism, against "the disobedient white church that had reduced African Americans to obsequious believers in their own spiritual inferiority and the right of whites to dictate the terms of religious faith."[103] If he had been alive in the 1960s, he probably would have been a Black Panther, because he believed and advocated that Blacks should not be defenseless in the face of white violence and oppression. He believed in armed Black self-defense, and at one church meeting, it had to be a shock to people when he placed two revolvers on top of his Bible and said, "My life depends on the word of God and these guns."[104] McNeal was the first person to seriously raise the issue of reparations for all the years Africans

---

102. Mary Frances Berry and John Blassingame, *Long Memory: The Black Experience in America* (New York: Oxford University Press, 1982), 108.

103. Wilmore, *Black Religion and Black Radicalism*, 152.

104. Whelchel, *The History and Heritage of African-American Churches*, 140.

spent in servitude. He was committed to the emigration of Blacks to Africa, and reparation money would be used for that purpose. No love was lost on this country for McNeal, and he was convinced this country would never do right by African Americans. He believed that in terms of reparations, Blacks were owed "forty billions of dollars."[105] Turner led a movement that included a "Blackenized form of the Christian faith that went far beyond anything that had developed out of the African American church . . . a reinterpreted belief system that was essentially radical in both its analysis of the Black condition and its programmatic solution to racism and oppression."[106]

Changes in the Black Church

With the assassination of President Lincoln and the elimination of all Black rights and privileges under Reconstruction, the Black Church found itself in the midst of the struggle to regain those rights guaranteed by the US Constitution and not return to the values embedded in the Constitution that Blacks were three-fifths—or less—of a human being. The Black Church was on the forefront of fighting to secure voting rights, which the South effectively stripped through poll taxes and literacy tests. The Black Church continued to fight for education for all Blacks, with several of the historically Black colleges and universities (HBCUs) started under the auspices of the Black Church. The Black Church was a loud voice against the belief that African Americans were by nature and DNA inferior and would never be able to participate in self-governing.[107]

In spite of enslavement, Jim Crow, segregation, and continued discrimination and death at the hands of the police, even when God has seemed absent, Black people have continued to pray, preach, and sing, invoking the glory of God. In spite of evidence to the contrary, Black faith kept hope alive even though it took four hundred years for freedom to become a semi-reality.[108] It could be said that Black Christian faith in the face of continued injustice and white Christian supremacy is beyond belief.

The unasked and unspoken question is this: Why do we continue to believe, to have faith?

---

105. Wilmore, *Black Religion and Black Radicalism*, 150.

106. Wilmore, *Black Religion and Black Radicalism*, 199.

107. Whelchel, *The History and Heritage of African-American Churches*, 147.

108. Harris, *Black Suffering*, 119.

My grandmother had another saying: "When you lie down with dogs, you get up with fleas." When you live among the oppressor, you pick up the prejudices of the oppressor, and if not ever-vigilant, the tactics used by whites to divide and conquer are adopted by the marginalized. The oppressed turn on themselves; they strive to be like the oppressor. This is how colorism found its way into the Black Church and Black society; it still exists today. As colonial Virginia moved to a slave society, rich and poor whites were bound together against an enslaved Black caste. Whiteness became the standard of who was human and who was not; who had rights and who did not. Prior to Bacon's Rebellion of 1675–1676, there had been English, French, African; after the rebellion, color was the determining factor in the social strata. The policing of caste was based on color.[109] "Black" became synonymous with "slave." With the rape of Blacks by white men and women, biracial children were born, and the degree of whiteness improved one's status. To be half-white was better than being all Black; however, being even half-white could not overcome being Black in an enslaving caste society.

Allegedly, the more whiteness one possessed, the better one was; therefore, colorism entered the slave society. Lighter Blacks were used for house duty; they were closer to whites in more ways than one. Darker Blacks were relegated to field duty. Those Blacks who worked in the enslaver's house felt superior to those who worked in the field. Those Blacks of a lighter hue believed they should have some if not all of the privileges accorded to whites. Certain Black churches catered to lighter-skinned Blacks who also adopted more of the Eurocentric customs and traditions. They looked down on the darker-skinned Blacks who might still favor the more emotional worship style. Rather than use the Negro spirituals, the churches attended by lighter-skinned Blacks used the anthems and hymns of the white church. They wanted to leave behind all vestiges of slavery.

The lighter-complexioned or elite Blacks of the post-Reconstruction era considered themselves genetically superior to Blacks with less white blood. White society propped up these lighter-skinned Blacks' delusion of superiority, and some actually believed that one day, white society would accept them as they adopted more and more of what they believed to be

---

109. Ned and Constance Sublette, *The American Slave Coast: A History of the Slave-Breeding Industry* (Chicago: Lawrence Hill Books, 2016), 133–35.

the civilizing attributes of whiteness. Cambridge educated, the Rev. Dr. Alexander Crummell, the founder of St. Luke's Episcopal Church in Washington, DC, believed—only to be disappointed—that because of his education and his demeanor as the perfect Victorian gentleman, he would be accepted in Washington's white society. During his time, Crummell was one of the most educated Black men in America; however, that would not improve his status in the eyes of whites. Even though he was of a darker complexion, he harbored color and caste prejudice, and he believed that Blacks would be hampered from being accepted in white society because too many Blacks were "ignorant, unkempt, dirty, animal-like, repulsive, and half-heathen—brutal and degraded."[110] It has to be remembered that Blacks had only been out of slavery for about ten years, emancipated without education, property, or a means to support themselves. Blacks engaged in internalized racial oppression and sought to distance themselves from other Blacks they deemed as beneath them. Even with the adoption of white values and an emerging caste system, the Black Church was still a force of immeasurable good in the Black community.

During the Harlem Renaissance, Alain Locke and W. E. B. Du Bois were among other African Americans and Caribbeans of African descent intellectuals who shaped a literary movement that was propelled by their desire to push a new agenda about Black culture—political agency—which would include a Black Jesus. The concept of a Black Jesus during the early twentieth century was no easier for whites to accept than it was when Bishop Henry McNeal Turner declared that God is Negro in the late nineteenth century. Continuing to forge a theology that pushed racist theology to the margins disrupted white supremacy and decentered Europe and whiteness. Reggie Williams writes, "The white Christ of the modern colonial construct was complicit in the race terror as an opiate Jesus who sedated Black people, convincing them to accept racism and sub-humanity as divinely ordained by God."[111] There is no authentic Jesus for those who are wedded to white supremacy, so white supremacists become idol worshipers. God's justice was on the side of the oppressed. For Williams, "Blackening Jesus helped African Americans to reimagine him outside the structures of white-supremacist religion."[112]

---

110. Wilson Jeremiah Moses, *Alexander Crummell: A Study of Civilization and Discontent* (New York: Oxford University Press, 1989), 209.

111. Williams, *Bonhoeffer's Black Jesus*, 54.

112. Williams, *Bonhoeffer's Black Jesus*, 62.

On the morning of September 15, 1963, a bomb destroyed the lives of four little Black girls, Denise McNair, Addie Mae Collins, Carol Robertson, and Cynthia Wesley, who had just finished Sunday school at the 16th Street Baptist Church in Birmingham, Alabama. In the explosion, the white face of Christ in one of the stained glass windows was blown out. Pictures and windows that contained a white Christ were not uncommon in Black churches or homes. But could this window, with the white face of the Jesus blown out with the rest of the window remaining intact, be an omen? James Baldwin and Reinhold Niebuhr struggled with its meaning. What did it mean that the white face of Jesus in a Black church had been destroyed? Baldwin wrote that the destruction of the white face was "an achievement" because Blacks had long been oppressed and victimized by "an alabaster Christ." The blown-out face presented an opportunity; if Christ had no face, Baldwin wrote, "We must give him a new face. Give him a new consciousness. And make the whole ideal, the whole hope, of Christian love a reality."[113] Whiteness had stolen the face of Christ and wrapped itself in it, thereby laying claim to white holiness. Whiteness became holy.[114] In hijacking Jesus, whiteness was able to market its hatred of Blacks, Jews, and Catholics by sending its white, blond, blue-eyed Jesus around the world.[115]

Black Women

While the advancement of Black theology was good news, there were problems, one of which was the lack of Black women's voices in the Black Church. It is highly problematic when those who are oppressed then become the oppressor. That is how internalized oppression works. The Black Church was rife with sexism. Women were denied ordination and leadership roles in the church, a problem that remains in some churches and denominations. The Bible had been used to deny the humanity of Black men (and women) by whites, and then Black men used the Bible to deny God's call on women.[116] We need only to look at the denial of

---

113. Edward J. Blum and Paul Harvey, *The Color of Christ: The Son of God and the Saga of Race in America* (Chapel Hill: University of North Carolina Press, 2012), 4.

114. Blum and Harvey, *The Color of Christ*, 9.

115. Blum and Harvey, *The Color of Christ*, 10.

116. James H. Cone, *For My People: Black Theology and the Black Church* (Maryknoll, NY: Orbis Books, 1984), 132.

ordination to Jarena Lee by Richard Allen. Although Allen fought for recognition in the white church (and society), which led to the founding of the first African American denomination, when Lee requested ordination, Allen denied her using the sexist church discipline of the Methodist Church, which Allen brought over to the African Methodist Episcopal (AME) Church.[117] As Black theology developed, Kelly Brown Douglas, Jacqueline Grant, and others challenged James Cone to consider the role of women in the church and Black theology, and they went on to create womanist theology, Black liberation theology for Black women.

It should not surprise, although it is disappointing, that the Black Church, born out of racial oppression, would then oppress women and restrict certain roles to only men, among them ordination and preaching. Here again is where history is important. When we go back to the founding of the Black Church, in traditional African cultures, women were not subordinate to men. Instead of inheritance and ancestry flowing from the father, many African traditions have matrilineal systems; that is, wealth and status in society depend on the mother. In some African traditions the Mother God, as opposed to Father God, is worshiped.[118] This begs the question: If certain African traditions were passed on to later generations in this country, even under the system of enslavement, how did the Black Church become sexist? The answer is fairly simple. American society was and is sexist, and women are viewed as being less capable, less worthy, less intelligent. For much of this country's history, women were viewed as property. As the Black Church became more embedded in American society, the men who controlled it adopted sexist ideas and beliefs about women, and those ideas and beliefs influenced Black men to oppress Black women. In addition to seeing how white and Black women were treated, Black men were also subject to plantation theology, hearing, "Slaves, obey your masters," "Wives, obey your husbands," and that women were to be silent in church. As much as Africans fought against white supremacy and ideals, they were still caught in the snare of assimilation and the adoption of European customs. As we see with Richard Allen, the full-scale adoption of the *Book of Discipline* of the Methodist Church

---

117. Whelchel, *The History and Heritage of African-American Churches*, 121. See also Bettye Collier-Thomas, *Daughters of Thunder: Black Women Preachers and Their Sermons, 1850–1979* (San Francisco: Jossey-Bass, 1998).

118. Whelchel, *The History and Heritage of African-American Churches*, 115.

was the norm, which denied ordination to women. In sum, slavery skewed gender roles for Blacks, and since Black men were emasculated by slavery and racism, there was a tendency to reserve the ministerial positions of power for themselves.[119] Women are still struggling in the church to be seen as called by God to positions of leadership. In the Black Church, the African Methodist Episcopal Zion (AMEZ) was the first to ordain a woman, Julia A. Forte, in 1894.

Black Worship

Black worship is as varied as Black religion. It includes emotional displays but is more than that. There is no one way to worship in the Black Church. The varied cultural foundations of Blacks throughout the diaspora are all on display in worship. Some are contained in a rigid order of service, while other expressions are guided by the Holy Spirit in all her glory. Some expressions result in the shout or the holy dance.[120] Worship in the Black Church is about empowerment. We come together as the gathered to become empowered to go back out into a racist and hostile world. Africans in America leave church to return to a world where at any moment, an agent of the state, the police officer, can execute the warrant of death, a warrant that is based on skin color. The gathering and the scattering is rooted in the New Testament; we gather, and then we scatter, to continue the work of Jesus Christ knowing that to challenge empire can result in death. We are empowered by the One who is empowered by God and who is our example of how to speak truth to power. This audacity, which is without limit and not restricted by any human convention, enables everyone to be who God has created them to be and enables all to do what God calls us to do. Black worship creates the world and life as it should be with the belief that it is in the here and now.[121] Therefore, Christian worship—all Christian worship—should begin grounded in the knowledge of God's divine intervention and empowerment by the Holy Spirit. Those assembled hear the word of God and then respond to the story of God in Jesus Christ by acting.[122]

---

119. Whelchel, *The History and Heritage of African-American Churches*, 119.

120. Cheryl J. Sanders, *Saints in Exile* (New York: Oxford University Press, 1996), 61.

121. Frederick Hilborn Talbot, *African American Worship: New Eyes for Seeing* (Eugene, OR: Wipf & Stock Publishers, 2007), 65.

122. Costen, *African American Worship*, 105.

This divine intervention is with the people of God regardless of what they call themselves, Christian or otherwise. This divine intervention was with the Africans long before they were forcefully torn from Mother Africa. The ground of Black worship is the understanding that in this moment there is a transformed relationship between the worshiper and the Creator. Everything is made new. To meet and be together so this transformation could take place, to experience this newness of life in the life, death, and resurrection of Jesus Christ, the enslaved were willing to risk violence and death. In the meeting and the worship experience, there was a both/and: there was a realized eschatology that looked toward a future life with Jesus and a new life, a different life of freedom in the here and now. There was the praising and thanking God as if the end-time moment had become a reality on earth. Preaching, as opposed to the Eucharist, has always been at the center of the Black Church, for it is in the preached word that hope is given to Black people—not a blind optimism but, again, the hope that they will be able to get through whatever happens, that God will give them strength, and that Jesus is in the suffering with them. They hear that they are loved by God their Creator. Liturgy is a conversation, liturgy is the work of the people, it is participation. The call-and-response of the Black Church can be traced to African culture. It reminds us of the relationship that exists between the preacher and the congregation[123] and the preacher and congregation with God.

When Black people had and *have* church, Jesus shows up in the breaking of the bread, in baptism, in the preaching and the singing. The Word *shows up*. And when the Word shows up, there will be the raising of holy hands, there will be dancing, and there will be the *hoop*, the intonation of Black preaching. When two or three of God's people show up, divine intervention occurs,[124] and there will be a change; there will be a new identity that will show on the face when one leaves the gathered and returns to the world ready to carry on with the mission of Jesus. It is in the midst of the gathered that "a glimmer of hope is seen in the midst of the struggle and suffering."[125] In the worship of Africans in America, the mystic Howard Thurman reminds us that for worship to be authentic, the entire body must be involved. The Holy Spirit takes over the whole body,

---

123. Talbot, *African American Worship*, 69.

124. James H. Cone, *Speaking the Truth* (Grand Rapids, MI: Eerdmans, 1986), 18–19.

125. Costen, *African American Worship*, 107.

and there is a move toward a new life. Now, this doesn't mean that the worries of life just disappear, because they don't. There might be outward signs of joy while the person is crying and hurt on the inside, but there is a mechanism to acknowledge the hurt, as it does with racism or violence, and then a way to deal with the hurt. We become the miracle we pray for to deal with the violence and abuse of racism. Worship must not be an opiate that merely dulls the pain for a while; worship must lift up the hurt and provide real-world solutions for their resolution. Involvement in Black worship involves the inculcation of a new identity that is bound up in the interaction with others and that the love of self and others is the visible manifestation of worshiping God.[126]

It is no wonder the enslavers were not enthused about the enslaved having church. It was in those gatherings the enslaved no longer saw themselves as property, chattel, things, nobodies; in those gatherings they saw themselves as the beloved children of God they were. It was in those gatherings during the struggle for civil rights, with the camp meetings in churches, that dehumanized Blacks gained the strength to face the whips, the rapes, the biting dogs, the fire hoses, and the Bull Connors. It was in those gatherings that change, *metanoia*, occurred—from being enslaved to free, from being nobody to becoming somebody. African spirituality in America was a religion of transformation, a religion of survival where a new social order is constructed and made real that facilitates acts of justice and even rebellion and insurrection.[127] In the sanctified church, when the saints are filled with the Holy Spirit, it is reminiscent of being possessed by the Spirit in the African tradition. The drums, cymbals, tambourines, saxophones, bass guitars, hands, and feet—the music of the saints—all produce a special sound that elicits shouts and screams. There is a bluesness to what is heard and experienced.[128]

Worship in the Black Church provides a womb in which the meaning of life is birthed and nurtured, and it flows from the community to the person. As indicated previously, Black worship is transformative; through worship, a new identity is formed, and the individual finds meaning in the context of the community.[129]

---

126. Battle, *The Black Church in America*, 67.

127. Costen, *African American Worship*, 108.

128. Young, *Pan-African Theology*, 108.

129. Battle, *The Black Church in America*, 29.

Worship leads to mission. We are the called, and we are sent out to take Jesus into a hurting world. When there is injustice and bondage, worshipers can be called to insurrection and rebellion against injustice and bondage, as demonstrated by Nat Turner, Denmark Vesey, Gabriel Prosser, Harriet Tubman, Diane Nash, Rosa Parks, Martin Luther King, Malcolm X, and the Black Lives Matter movement. They represent for the oppressed empowered engagement in the struggle for freedom. Church was outside the building where white supremacy was destroying the lives of Black people. This reminds us that worship is more than performing rituals. The walls between the sacred and the secular are torn down just as Jesus was at the intersection of heaven and earth. Further, in Romans 12 the apostle Paul is quite clear that worship extends beyond the walls of the gathered and that rituals must not be oversacramentalized because they can become the main focus as opposed to transforming unjust structures that deny the humanity of all God's people. The work of the people, the liturgy, that extends beyond the boundaries of the gathered, lifts up the life, death, and resurrection of Jesus; this is the central mark of liturgy. The gathered embrace and then demonstrate the need to "go forth into the world to love and serve" in spite of the fact that the world and the worshiper are not always compassionate and loving.[130]

The Power of Song

As discussed earlier, music is important in worship. It is not a filler in the liturgy; it is not for entertainment. It is a vital part of the liturgy. In traditional African religions, music always includes dancing. There was no difference between music and dancing; they were one in the same.[131] For the enslaver, their fear of singing by the enslaved was justified, especially since the enslavers learned that the songs could contain subtle messages. To have all their bondspeople singing at the same time was an act of rebellion. Singing was empowering; it permitted the enslaved to transcend their owners' power over them, and enslavers who permitted Africans to create their own songs were inviting insurrection. Songs had both a here-and-now and an otherworldly focus.

---

130. Costen, *African American Worship*, 111–13.

131. Lincoln and Mamiya, *The Black Church in the African American Experience*, 353.

Like preaching, when songs had an otherworldly focus, the enslaved imagined the time when they would be free in the present.[132] The enslaved were prohibited from singing some songs because the enslavers figured out their double meaning. Songs like "Ride on, King Jesus," "No Man Can Hinder Me," or "Climbing Jacob's Ladder" exhibited rebellion against the enslaver's power over the African or showed that while it might take time, there would be a time when the enslaved would no longer be under the enslaver's control. The song "Don't You Get Weary" imagined a time when they would all walk together—that spirit of African community—and the enslaved would be free in the promised land, either in the North or in heaven. The songs confirmed that the enslaved had a choice when it might seem that they had no choice.[133] While death was an ever-present reality, the Africans also sang about not fearing death; they could take their own lives rather than submit to the deathly punishment of the enslaver, or they could wait until death came to them. Although enslaved, Africans exhibited they had a choice over life and death.[134] The subversiveness of the songs would spread through the house or the field; the people's dignity would not be taken. They sang "I hold up my brudder wid a tremblin' hand," symbolizing dignity in walking upright with an unbowed head, which was antithetical to the posture required by the enslaver.[135] "O Freedom," a spiritual that also became a protest song during the civil rights era, must have cast fear in the hearts of any enslaver.

O Freedom, O Freedom
O Freedom, over me,
And before I'll be a slave,
I'll be buried in my grave,
And go home to my Lord
And be free . . .

In antebellum society, the worth of Blacks was only as beasts of burden, and the spirituals countered that narrative. The spirituals defiantly

132. Riggins R. Earl Jr., *Dark Symbols, Obscure Signs: God, Self, and Community in the Slave Mind* (Knoxville: University of Tennessee Press, 2003), 74.

133. Earl, *Dark Symbols, Obscure Signs*, 74–76

134. Earl, *Dark Symbols, Obscure Signs*, 83.

135. Earl, *Dark Symbols, Obscure Signs*, 89.

said, "I matter. We matter. We are created in God's image. We are God's own." Not only were the songs acts of resistance, but they built community. Every voice was important; the call-and-response leadership was shared; everyone could participate. Singing was an act of democracy.[136] To study the music of the enslaved is to learn how they Africanized Christianity as residents in a strange and hostile land. The music was ecumenical, transcending any denominational structure, and rose out of Black suffering, sorrows, and a search for freedom under inhumane conditions. The songs of the enslaved gave "to the Christian faith a modern glossolalia" in which the enslavers' words were negated and those of the Bible made real.[137]

What Happened?

Somewhere along the trajectory of what it is to be the Black Church, something happened. After the civil rights era and the assassination of Martin Luther King Jr., the Black Church lost something; it lost its soul. It assimilated to whiteness, the white Church, and white Christianity. Unfortunately, when a movement or a religion depends on the strength of a person or a particular church, when that person dies, the Church can lose its direction and energy. In the early twentieth century, that is exactly what happened. With the death of Bishop Henry McNeal Turner in 1915, there was no one with his temperament or his boldness to step in to lead. As Gayraud Wilmore writes, there was no one who "combined the acuity of a theologian with the passion of an indefatigable Pan-African activist." No one "had the grass-roots following or audacity of Turner."[138] Turner's death left a void as race relations in the country worsened, and the Black Church shrunk back from the hard line of Turner and turned away from radical strategies of resistance and confrontation. Neither the Niagara Movement nor the National Association for the Advancement of Colored People (NAACP) was able to step in with the in-your-face passion of Turner. The focus was more accommodationist in the mold of Booker T. Washington, and colorism

---

136. Eileen Guenther, *In Their Own Words: Slave Life and the Power of Spirituals* (St. Louis: Morningstar Music Publishers, 2016), xviii–xix.

137. J. Alfred Smith Jr., "The Ecumenical Nature of African American Church Music," in *African American Heritage Hymnal* (Chicago: GIA Publications, 2001), 1–3.

138. Wilmore, *Black Religion and Black Radicalism*, 166.

allowed some Blacks to enter into fields and positions that were previously closed to them. It was a time when Black groups that advocated for equality became moderate in their approach to social change. White orthodox Christianity also loomed large, and the Black Church fell asleep as it attempted to imitate the white Church's example of what authentic Christian faith should be. The Black Church turned inward[139] and would not come out of its shell until Martin Luther King Jr. picked up the mantle. Joseph Washington, in writing about the deradicalization of the Black Church, offers:

> In that era of decline in the quest for freedom, the Negro minister remained the spokesman for the people with this difference—faced by unsurmountable obstacles, he succumbed to the cajolery and bribery of the white power structure and became its foil. Instead of freedom he preached moralities and emphasized rewards in the life beyond. . . . From this point on, the Black contribution lay dormant while the white contribution was active and dominating.[140]

The Black Church was not dead as Eddie Glaude Jr. later announced, but it was certainly anemic. It had been infected with the status quo of white Christianity. Still, all the blame cannot be placed on Black ministers. Then, as now, with the downward trend in church membership, secularization has its pull. Blacks of all classes desired what white society had and were willing to give up the radical nature of the Black Church to achieve what E. Franklin Frazier called the "Black Bourgeoisie."[141] The Black Church was becoming middle class and veering away from the religion that had kept the enslaved alive and hopeful.[142]

The Black Church, invisible and visible, even when it seems that it has lost its way, has always been about the beloved community. For Martin Luther King Jr., the beloved community was the goal; it was the organizing principle for his thought and activities. It was with King that the radical movement of the Black Church switched from the African

---

139. Kelly Miller, *Radicals and Conservatives: And Other Essays on the Negro in America* (1908; repr., New York: Schocken, 1968), 147–65.

140. Joseph R. Washington Jr., *Black Religion* (Boston: Beacon, 1964), 35.

141. E. Franklin Frazier, *The Black Bourgeoisie* (New York: Simon & Schuster, 1957).

142. James H. Cone, *Black Theology and Black Power* (New York: Seabury, 1969), 103–15.

Methodist Episcopal Church and Bishop Henry McNeal Turner to the Baptist Church. Although King did not begin as a radical, he became one. King could have led a comfortable life for the times. When he was called to pastor Dexter Avenue Baptist Church in Montgomery, Alabama, he never imagined the call that was about to be put upon his life. His pedigree was impeccable: he attended the right (and white) schools, and he had a doctorate. He had "everything he would need for a successful if prosaic career as a privileged, pampered minister of a fashionable, middle-class congregation in a capital of the Black South."[143] Joseph R. Washington describes King: "He had that Baptist hum which makes what is said only as important as how it is said."[144] King had that Black preaching style; he could moan and hoop. He could preach to the high and the low. His command of the English language and his education could take the congregation from the cotton fields of Alabama to the Greek temples of Athens. He could have led a simple pastor's life, but that was not to be. In December 1955, when Rosa Parks refused to let whiteness control her life anymore and refused to give up her seat on the bus, a seat she had paid for like any white person, King knew he would have to leave the safety of the pulpit and go to the streets, where the church was waiting for him. He knew he would be called to trouble both the waters and the white folk. He knew a target would be placed on his back and that he just might end up as one of those strange fruit about which jazz singer Billie Holiday had shocked the country with her soaring vocal tones.

Later, from a Birmingham jail, King would write of his own transformation from the comfortable Baptist pastor to the radical who was called to lay down his life for his friend. In his letter, he both critiqued and challenged the church. He wrote of a time when Christians were willing to suffer for what they believed and the church pushed to change society. He wrote of a time when Christians were a threat to those in power and were called "disturbers of the peace." He likened the early Christians to the civil rights workers who were called "outside agitators." Somewhere along the line, the Christian church lost the troublemaker who ended up on a cross on a hill: Jesus, who had to be killed because he was a threat to the status quo. The church, according to King, was weak and had no voice to which

---

143. Wilmore, *Black Religion and Black Radicalism*, 204.

144. Washington, *Black Religion*, 3.

anyone would listen.[145] Unfortunately, King's words ring true today; the church seems to be more concerned with maintaining itself than risking the cross.

King would go on to challenge the white power structure of this country and, ultimately, the federal government itself, and it would cost him his life. But even his brand of Christianity would later fall short as he was challenged by folk who looked like him. At the time of his death Blacks and whites disapproved of his message and direction. However, he led and pushed the church and ultimately ushered in the Black Power era and a different kind of Black Church, because he made Black Americans aware that they did not have to accept their lot in life and could change this country.

As we look to the future, the Black Church is called to continue to be the reservoir of Black culture in its many forms and to show examples of resistance and independence.[146] The Black Church will be different; it will be different because it has to be different if it is to remain relevant. The Covid-19 pandemic has shown that the church does not need the building; the church has been pushed outside where it belongs—among the people, among the dispossessed, among the marginalized. The Black Church is not dead; it has just left the building.

Reflection Questions

1. What do you know of the history of the Black Church, even if you attend a Black Church?

2. When you read that Western Christianity is racist, what feelings are engendered?

3. Is your church or parish predominantly white, Black, or multiracial/multicultural? Did you choose your church because of its racial makeup?

4. Why do you need to believe in God, Jesus, the church?

---

145. Martin Luther King Jr., "Letter from a Birmingham Jail," in Cornel West, ed., *The Radical King* (Boston: Beacon Press, 2015), 143.

146. Lincoln and Mamiya, *The Black Church in the African American Experience*, 15.

In Their Own Words

Female Clergy

We have to have these conversations, we have to have these discussions because—what was it that I saw recently? . . . Racism is so instilled in America that when people protest racism, they think that America itself is being protested. You know, that really says something; that's a really deep thought. I'm just happy that I'm going to be in a position where I get to give a sermon. I could be in the liliest-white parish in the country; I'm getting in the pulpit, and yes, I may get up there and talk about something that makes some people squirm in their seats, but I'm hoping people will understand who I am and the fact that my life is built on my spirituality and in my beliefs and that they will be able to listen and accept what I have to say. So that is one of my hopes as well because there's a lot of work to be done, a lot of work, so much work to be done.

Male Clergy

When asked about traditional Episcopal liturgy and African liturgy . . . I want both, and I love both, and really, I need both, and preferably at the same time. If it has to be in shifts: low church, Black gospel one Sunday and another Sunday, high-church Anglican, whether that's Afro Caribbean or otherwise. One of the best liturgical experiences I've ever had was in 2014. I got to spend three weeks at St. Nicholas Seminary in Ghana doing some research. I got to worship—I'll never forget this—at the cathedral in Cape Coast. The acolytes could have been trained by the Marines. It was the ceremonial, the military band. There was incense, and there was the Ghanaian prayer book; it's similar to the 1662, with the traditional language. If you could close your ears, and you were only looking visually, you would think that you were in very high church, a very Anglican church, similar to the Afro-Caribbean style. But then if you close your eyes, and only listen with your ears, you would think that you were in a very, kind of low church, very charismatic, energetic. The women were playing drums, and the people were swaying and singing, dancing, and the offerings were brought up. The women brought forward the baskets on their heads with the grain and things that they had collected, and it was a real offering. People bringing things they had grown on their land. It wasn't just the plate being passed around. If I could ever replicate something like that on American soil, I think I would be the happiest priest in the world.

Female Clergy

The only thing that mattered to me was finding an Episcopal Church. That was it. I didn't care, black or white. It was more for me about whether I felt welcome. I never even thought about a white or Black Episcopal Church, even though I grew up in predominantly Black Episcopal churches.

Female Clergy

I actually feel more comfortable in a white Episcopal Church now at this point in my life. There's a church. I'm sure you're familiar. Everybody knows about the African Episcopal Church of St. Thomas. There are things there I don't necessarily appreciate. I love my own culture, my African American culture. I am my authentic self every day. I love the liturgy, but I don't necessarily think that those two things have to be married together all the time. I love *LEVAS* (*Lift Every Voice and Sing*)—don't get me wrong, I want to see *LEVAS* in a church. But I don't want drums in the church. I don't want praise dancing in the church. I don't want some of the things of the Black Church and related to that culture.

CHAPTER FOUR

DISCIPLES OF JESUS
OR (WHITE) CLONES?

Unless you know your cultural context, you become potentially a pawn on the chessboard in the way we function within the structures of the church. And one of the things I always say to young Black priests is do not remove yourself from your cultural place because if you do, and you are unfortunate enough to get chewed up by the system, you have nothing to go back to.

—Canon Eve Pitts, Church of England

Devotees of the dominant nationalist Christianity are not known by the God of creation, for they instead have clung to the illusion of the God of white supremacy . . . those who exist on the underside of white Christianity must have absolutely nothing to do with this white God, white Christ, white church, white ritual, or white spirituality. . . . White Christianity refers to a worldview that embraces the supremacy of whiteness and believers in their manifest destiny of white bodies to occupy the highest echelons of power, profits, and privilege due solely to a light skin hue. . . . A white Christian worldview can be advocated by those who are Black or Brown, Jew or Muslim, queer or heteronormative, atheist or humanist—anyone who defends the current unjust and unholy political, economic, and social power struggles.

—Miguel A. De La Torre,
Decolonizing Christianity: Becoming Badass Believers

What does it mean to be Black and Catholic? It means that I come to my Church fully functioning. That doesn't frighten you, does it? I come to my Church fully functioning. I bring myself, my Black self, all that I am, all that I have, all that I hope to become. I bring my whole history, my traditions, my experience, my culture, my African-American song and dance and gesture and movement and teaching and preaching and healing and responsibility as a gift to the Church.

—Sister Thea Bowman, Franciscan Sisters of Perpetual Adoration

We consider something of the journey to ordination. We look at the identity that is jettisoned to join the (Club) . . . what it means to become empty of one's identity.

—A. D. A. France-Williams, *Ghost Ship: Institutional Racism and the Church of England*

But the hour is coming, and is now here, when true worshipers will worship the Father in spirit and truth, for the Father seeks such as these to worship him. God is Spirit, and those who worship him must worship in spirit and truth.

—John 4:23–24

Who are we forming with our preaching, teaching, and ministries: disciples of Jesus committed to his transformative mission, or Anglicans/Episcopalians clothed in whiteness. In 2020 the Rev. Katie Nakamura Renger spoke at a conference sponsored by the New Community of the Episcopal Church. In her presentation she asked, "Is there a place for me?" As an Asian American, does she have to leave who she is at the door to worship and to lead worship in an Episcopal space?

On Saturday, January 30, 2021, the Rt. Rev. Diana Akiyama was ordained and consecrated as the eleventh bishop of the Episcopal Diocese of Oregon. Bishop Akiyama is the first Japanese American woman ordained priest in the Episcopal Church, and she is the first Asian American woman consecrated as bishop. Pictures of her vestments flooded Facebook. As I looked at these photos, I noticed something different about them. Yes, they were the traditional vestments, chasuble, cope, miter, and the stole bishops have worn for eons, but there was something different about her vestments. As I studied them, mesmerized, I thought of the word *feminine*, but that wasn't quite right. As comments on the photos poured in, using words such as *exquisite* and *beautiful*, the words that came to me were *soft*, *light*. As if the Holy Spirit had descended upon her as a dove and she heard the words, "My daughter, I am well pleased." Here was a person whose people had also endured the hatred of this country, with the signing of Executive Order 9066 on February 19, 1942, during World War II, which authorized the U.S. military to forcefully remove Japanese citizens and residents on the west coast and treat them as enemies of this country. Her people had everything taken away from them and then were placed in internment camps because of fear of the "Other." And yet she and her people had survived, and now she is a bishop in the Episcopal Church, a church that has always feared the Other.

As she stood, arms outstretched in the picture, Bishop Diana looked as if she could take flight. I thought about the vestments of other bishops, male and female, and while they were colorful, they also appeared heavy, as if they would weigh down the wearers, as if the weight of the office was carried in the vestments, pressing down on them. But with Bishop Diana's, the cope flowed from her shoulders. It draped as a mother hen softly protects the hope of the next generation. The water pictured on the back of her cope flowed in a direction that is not usual. It flowed from the bottom—from a pool and up—to the right shoulder. As described by the creator of the garment, the water flowed up to the heavens. Heaven and earth met; heaven and earth meet in the person of Jesus. She looked as if she would take flight. The waters of baptism, Jesus's and ours, Bishop Diana carried on her shoulders, but she was not weighed down. The miter was not a crown, an emblem of empire; it was not oversized; it was not prominent. Rather, it was, like the colors of her vestments, subdued. The miter was a sign of her anointing as the ultimate of God's creation. The woman, who was created out of the first human (Adam), was the last—the ultimate—to be created by God; the pinnacle of God's creation. The images on the miter were that of a temple gate; the gate was chosen because it represents the "way"—Jesus is the way. Out of the deprivation suffered by her people, out of hatred of her people, out of the death of her people, she carried the hope that is Jesus with her. On the chasuble were the crests of two families, hers and another, the only two families of Japanese descent who attended St. Mark's Hood River Episcopal Church in Oregon. The crests tell an ancestral story. Our ancestral stories remind us whence we come and whose we are. All of her vestments were created using a traditional Japanese stencil technique called *katazome*, which represents nature—God's creative activity. When looking closely at the vestments, you could see elements of the earth and sea and air, elements in nature, themes from Oregon and her native Hawai'i. There were no lambs; no crowns; no Chi Rho, Constantine's battle standard. Her vestments spoke of life and not death. They did not speak of empire; they spoke of God's reign here on earth.[1]

---

1. Diocese of Oregon, "The Ordination and Consecration of the Rt. Rev. Diana D. Akiyama," January 30, 2021, *https://www.pbs.org/show/Black-church/*.

Bishop Akiyama's vestments and Rev. Renger's plea remind us that while we are Episcopalian, we are not required to fit in a prescribed box—that we should be free to bring all of who we are to this branch of the Jesus Movement. The Very Rev. Dr. Kelly Brown Douglas, in the PBS documentary *The Black Church: The Is Our Story, This Is Our Song*, tells of how she was about to leave the Church until she was taught by James Cone that she could be Black and Christian, Black and Episcopal.[2] How are we who are not white being formed as Episcopalians, and what is the effect?

The Centers for Disease Control and Prevention (CDC) has announced that racism is a public health issue, that racism kills.[3] The centuries of denial of humanity, of white terrorism, of discrimination that have been embedded in every aspect of American life all coalesce to affect the health outcomes of African Americans in ways that are disproportionate compared to other racial groups. The Church is one of these systems. We have acknowledged that the American Christian church, built on the foundation of white supremacy, through its acts of commission and omission, has, since before this land was the United States, been involved in the denial of human rights for Africans (and others) in America. The Church is racist, and if racism kills, the Church, the Episcopal Church, is killing us. The longer we stay and adhere to Eurocentric styles of worship, doctrines, and beliefs, we Africans in America are participating in our own deaths—a slow death that sneaks up and snuffs out life.

The deaths caused by the Church might not be physical. As the CDC offers, the effects of racism on health outcomes result in over two hundred unnecessary deaths of Blacks in this country every day, but there are also deaths of the soul, of the spirit, of personhood; we are erased. This should not come as a surprise, because ever since Black people asserted our personhood, that we are created by and in the image of God, whiteness has participated in the slow onslaught of Black genocide. Systemic racism structures societal opportunities and assigns value to people based on phenotype: how people look, the color of skin.[4] The mere fact that

---

2. Henry Louis Gates, *The Black Church: This Is Our Story, This Is Our Song*, PBS, *https://www.pbs. org/show/Black-church/*.

3. Centers for Disease Control and Prevention, "Racism and Health: Racism Is a Serious Threat to the Public's Health," last reviewed July 8, 2021, *https://www.cdc.gov/healthequity/racism-disparities/ index.html*.

4. Camara Phyllis Jones, "Confronting Institutionalized Racism," *Phylon* 50, no. 1/2 (2002): 7–22, *https://doi.org/10.2307/4149999*.

some Africans in America have spent centuries and resources attempting to assimilate and look white through surgery, skin lightening, and marrying light or white, or passing shows the deleterious effect of racism and whiteness on those for whom God has created and to whom God has given Black skin. Racism is trauma, trauma is individualized, and trauma has been an integral part of Black–white relationships since the first Africans were taken from the shores of Africa.[5] As with complaints of discrimination filed with governmental or local agencies, the trauma is compounded by the fact that the dominant white culture demands evidence of the trauma before it will accept the woundedness experienced. There is a lack of sensitivity to the trauma experienced by Black people living in a racist society and participating in a racist church. The testimony of African Americans is disregarded because whites have no frame of reference.[6]

Camara Jones and David Williams have shared the need for American society, in all aspects, to overcome "the somnolence of racism denial [and] dismantle the system of racism, and put in its place a system in which all people can thrive."[7] It would seem that the Church, which claims to be the body of Christ, would be the starting place for that dismantling by first confessing and repenting in real ways that racism continues to exist in the pews.

Again, we must return to W. E. B. Du Bois as we look at the physical and spiritual health of our Black siblings and the role the Church must play. In his 1899 book *Philadelphia Negro*, Du Bois wrote, "The most difficult social problem in the matter of Negro health is the peculiar attitude of the nation toward the well-being of the race. There have been few other cases in the history of civilized peoples where human suffering has been viewed with such peculiar indifference."[8] While Du Bois was writing in particular about the physical health of the Black community, as we acknowledge that racism kills, David Williams suggests that there is an "empathy gap"; that is, groups of people are able to empathize with the suffering of those within one's own group but not with others in different

---

5. Resmaa Menakem, *My Grandmother's Hands: Racialized Trauma and the Pathway to Mending Our Hearts and Bodies* (Las Vegas: Central Recovery Press, 2017), 43, 61.

6. Dan Hauge, "The Trauma of Racism and the Distorted White Imagination," in Stephanie N. Areal and Shelly Rambo, eds., *Post-Traumatic Public Theology* (London: Palgrave Macmillan, 2016), 94.

7. Harvard Radcliffe Institute, "Naming Racism," June 4, 2020, *https://www.radcliffe.harvard.edu/event/2020-naming-racism-virtual*.

8. W. E. B. Du Bois, *The Philadelphia Negro: A Social Study* (Philadelphia: University of Pennsylvania Press, 1996), 163.

groups. It may be asked why is this important, especially for the church, which is supposed to be different than the world, the society, in which it operates. According to Williams, when empathy is lacking for a group of people, their pain is not felt, and little support exists for policies or laws that would relieve their suffering. The ideology of inferiority, Williams continues, is ". . . pervasive in the norms, values, symbols, language and assumptions of the ['in' group] and they shape attitudes, values, stereotypes, behaviors, social policies and institutions."[9] If the church is to be the body of Christ, if it is to be and show Jesus to a hurting world, it would seem that it would take seriously the charge of Winnie Varghese, a priest in the Episcopal Church, who writes, "Whiteness is a tool of racism, whiteness is a tool of white supremacy, all kinds of whiteness are possible. . . . Whiteness is a claim to power, it's a claim to rightness, it's a racialized claim and there is no such thing as being white and being a Christian; you have to resist that identity."[10]

Formed for What?

When does or should the formation of faithful adults begin, and what is the role of the church in that formation? How do we form disciples of Christ with all their cultural beauty and not merely as clones of whiteness? James Fowler writes of a 1979 presentation made by Walter Brueggemann, "Covenanting as Human Vocation," which offered several insights that lend themselves to this discussion of adult faith formation. Brueggemann stated that viewing adults shaped for covenant living "transposes all identity questions into vocational questions."[11] These questions move along a continuum of questions from "Who am I?" to "Whose am I?" to "Who am I in relation to all these significant others in whose eyes I see myself reflected?" to "Who am I in relation to the Creator, Ruler, Redeemer-Liberator of the universe?"[12] There should be no one "correct" answer to any of the questions, with the exception of "Whose am I?," because we are all different even though we call ourselves Episcopalians.

---

9. Harvard Radcliffe Institute, "Naming Racism."

10. France-Williams, *Ghost Ship*, 14.

11. Walter Brueggemann, "Covenanting as Human Vocation," *Interpretation* 33, no. 2 (1979): 115–29, qtd. in James Fowler, *Becoming Adult, Becoming Christian: Adult Development and Christian Faith* (San Francisco: Jossey-Bass, 2000), 7.

12. Fowler, *Becoming Adult, Becoming Christian*, 75.

Americans are becoming less religious; however, that does not mean that people are not spiritual or don't believe in God. What is known is that people who may or may not be affiliated with a specific faith tradition often decide which aspects of a religion or practice they will adopt. They feel free to disregard certain aspects of a tradition and to bring in aspects of others. They are willing to blur the boundaries between beliefs to find something that speaks to their specific needs, to fit together a combination of beliefs, traditions, or rituals that speaks to them and engages their entire being. As an example, former NBA player Joakim Noah wears a Christian crucifix and uses Muslim prayer beads and Tibetan Buddhist stones; he says he is a little bit of everything.[13]

The number of those who belong or adhere to multiple belief systems will probably increase in the future, and they are part of this country's dynamic religious landscape.[14] For many, this would be syncretism; however, as Tara Isabella Burton writes in *Strange Rites: New Religions for a Godless World*, syncretism is not new and has long been part of American immigrant traditions. She specifically looks to Afro-Caribbean adherents of voodoo and other folk religions, as well as Mexican folk traditions mixed with Catholicism. Rather than creating new religions, Burton writes, people are mixing traditions on a personal level that may or may not be known to others.[15] This mixing and fluidity occur because people are not tied to doctrines or creeds, and they "hunger for a spiritual identity and surrounding community that precisely reflects their values, their moral and social institutions, their lived experience, and their sense of self."[16] When a faith tradition or religion fails to value one's personhood and to acknowledge the *imago Dei*, one will either leave that tradition or modify it to uphold one's selfhood. Underlying all of this is an unspoken question: Who says? Paul, early church fathers (and mothers) and modern theologians are all human beings. None are divine. Their doctrines and systematic categorizing are all part of figuring out this faith thing. It is, as attributed to St. Anselm, truly faith seeking understanding. We want to understand, so we keep pushing, we keep questioning, we keep

---

13. Duane R. Bidwell, *When One Religion Isn't Enough: The Lives of the Spiritually Fluid* (Boston: Beacon Press, 2018), 2.

14. Yonat Shimron, "Embodying the Future of Faith," *Washington Post*, August 15, 2020, B2.

15. Tara Isabella Burton, *Strange Rites: New Religions for a Godless World* (New York: Public Affairs, 2020), 23.

16. Burton, *Strange Rites*, 24.

adding. If we merely accepted the early church fathers and, for example, European theologians, we wouldn't have liberation theology, Black liberation theology, womanist theology, queer theology, and others. But we keep pushing.

How God was "sought" in the first century CE is different than how people seek God in the twenty-first century. How oppressed people seek God is different than those who have not lived their lives under the yoke of oppression. If we are not comfortable with the questions and the pushing because they challenge long-held and ancient beliefs, the church will continue to be irrelevant for those who seek brave space to see and be themselves. This irrelevancy could lead to what Jeffrey C. Pugh calls a religionless Christianity. This form of Christianity would reclaim its prophetic voice and refuse to continue to be a chaplain to the nation's political machine. Christianity would be free of doctrines and prescribed rituals and would free itself from its domestication by the state. It would use its voice, risk all, and become a "countervailing sign to the world" that racism will end and God's reign will be a reality in the here and now.[17]

Who Forms?

If done intentionally, Christian formation occurs from the womb to the tomb. We are constantly being formed as disciples of Jesus. If we have formed parents as disciples, they begin to think about how to raise the child in the faith while the child is still in utero. If we are intentional about formation, our elders are still in the process of learning, becoming disciples regardless of age. For example, for many older Black Americans, the church is the primary and sometimes only organization to which they belong. The church has been a shelter in the storm of life and of racism, and many carry the trauma and the woundedness from years of dealing with racism. The church was the place where their personhood was valued when it wasn't valued in society. It was the place where they had power over their lives when that power was missing in society.

The "we-consciousness" of the Black Church acts as an extended family, particularly as family members and friends die. This extended family assists the elders in navigating continued oppression, life's trials

---

17. Jeffrey C. Pugh, *Religionless Christianity: Dietrich Bonhoeffer in Troubled Times* (New York: T&T Clark International, 2008), 150–51.

and tribulations, and spiritual woundedness. The Black congregation engages in what Anne Wimberly calls "soul care." Soul care involves the belief in the sacredness of persons, which harkens back to Africa and African caring traditions. From formal formation practices to worship in which the elders join with others in God's presence to lift up their joys and to praise God and obtain guidance, there should be opportunity for extemporaneous prayer and testimony that give life to their lived experience.[18]

End-of-life issues must also be considered. Churches are very good at celebrating homegoing services; however, the preparation for death, other than sessions on wills and other legal documents and making the church a financial beneficiary, is sometimes left in the shadows. As elders age, they may have questions about death. How do you explain it in a way that makes sense to someone who might take the Bible literally, with some biblical people living for centuries, and yet we are limited to three score and ten? How do we really explain resurrection since, as my grandmother always said, no one ever came back to tell, and when the imperative to "have faith" is not enough?

Understanding the difference between African American men and women is critical to designing formation processes. As men age, one of the major issues concerns an evaluation of how well they have lived their lives according to God and whether God is pleased with them. For many older Black women, they do not need to have their lives affirmed by their religious leader; they are able to exude confidence in how they have lived their lives, and if not, they are able to let it go. They tend to be more confident that God has gotten them to where they are and that God will continue to take them the rest of the way.[19]

We form disciples of Jesus through formal education or indoctrination, through our preaching, liturgy, music, and mission. So, the question that begs an answer is whether we are forming disciples or white Episcopalians. It is only because of a lack of imagination that we cannot see formation more broadly than one-size-fits-all.

---

18. Anne E. Streaty Wimberly, "Congregational Care in the Lives of Black Older Adults," in Melvin A. Kimble and Susan H. McFadden eds., *Aging, Spirituality, and Religion*, vol. 2 (Minneapolis: Fortress Press, 2003), 101–3.

19. Christie Cozad Neuger, "Does Gender Influence Late-Life Spiritual Potentials?," in Kimble and McFadden, eds., *Aging, Spirituality, and Religion*, vol. 2, 67.

Liturgy—the Work of the People—as Formation

Liturgy is more than what happens on Sunday in the worship service. Liturgy, the work, goes beyond the dismissal into a world that sometimes acts as if God does not exist. It is in this context that liturgy becomes liberative. Liturgy is about freedom—freedom from oppressive systems and freedom to be all God has intended us to be. We come together; we gather together in this primary symbol of unity to hear the word of God proclaimed, to share a sacred meal, to be fed by the body of Christ, to be strengthened, and then to be sent out into that same yet different world that turned its back on Jesus and killed him. We don't gather for our own sake; we gather for the sake of those who still need to know the liberating love of the One who came so we could have life here on this earth and have it more abundantly. At its core, the Black religious experience is education. Religion—its practices, doctrines, disciplines—constitutes education at its elemental level.

For Blacks in a hostile and dehumanizing situation, learning for formation must be liberating; it must free those who seek its message from the brainwashing of white Christian preachers and educators intent on maintaining their society's position of superiority. This poses another question: How does an institution that can be viewed as subversive (the invisible institution) and that seeks to dismantle the teachings of the dominant society work within and yet outside of those existing dominant structures?

As we learn the history of religion, or Christianity, in America as it concerned Blacks, it has been one of working against the word of God, a denial that all are created in the image of God. A system had to be created in which the being White is seen as being better and the oppressed aspire to become White, contributing to their own oppression. Socialization occurs in all social environments and has a negative effect when another's culture is seen as superior to one's own. Education, whether informal or formal, and including religious education, is either for liberation or to maintain domination.[20] Failure to provide adequate educational opportunities (through all aspects of the religious experience) can result in either (1) the complete assimilation of the other culture that creates an environment where one's own cultural values are negatively viewed, or (2) a culture is adopted that is opposed to African-centered values that are critical

20. Charles R. Foster and Fred Smith, *Black Religious Experience: Conversations on Double Consciousness and the Work of Grant Shockley* (Nashville: Abingdon Press, 2003), 62.

to the Black family.[21] Survival of Black people is dependent on the protection of the extended family, both intimate and church, and the bridging of the boundaries of class and status.[22] Without cultural and historical grounding, Black people find themselves the victims of a church that creates Anglican (white) clones. A positive religious experience can counter these negative societal effects.

Models of Freedom

Since education undergirds any religious experience, in assessing religious education and formation proposals, we must remember that approaching the Black experience beginning with slavery in this country does not take advantage of the African insights into the collective human experience or the theological understandings that can enhance Black Americans' quality of life both inside and outside the church. Therefore, it is important to remember that Africentrism refers to the "practice of examining historical evidence as well as current reality by utilizing pre-colonial Black African rather than European civilization, expansionism, and colonial activity as major points of reference."[23] It is important to Black Americans' self-worth to be able to perceive the world from an African-oriented center. This produces a new consciousness of one's own humanity.[24] Following are three models of formation by Grant Shockley, Lora-Ellen McKinney, and Anne Wimberly that support that African-oriented center.

Grant Shockley shares his Intentional Engagement Model, which is based on a social justice ministry approach, which was successful in the era of the civil rights struggle, and had potential for adaptation to churches in the early 1990s. To employ it today, its adaptation requires that the church be grounded in the need for social justice—in reality, God's justice—in society, for it is a model that relates mission to ministry.[25] This model has five

---

21. Jacqueline Grant, "A Theological Framework," in *Working with Black Youth: Opportunities for Christian Ministry*, ed. Charles R. Foster and Grant S. Shockley (Nashville, TN: Abingdon Press, 1992), 64.

22. Romney M. Moseley, "Retrieving Intergenerational and Intercultural Faith," in Charles R. Foster and Grant S. Shockley, eds., *Working with Black Youth: Opportunities for Christian Ministry* (Nashville: Abingdon Press, 1992), 83.

23. Ronald Edward Peters, "Africentrism as a Challenge to Contemporary Christian Ministry," in Ronald Edward Peters and Marsha Snulligan Haney, eds., *Africentric Approaches to Christian Ministry: Strengthening Urban Congregations* (Lanham, MD: University Press of America, 2006), 36–37.

24. Peters, "Africentrism as a Challenge to Contemporary Christian Ministry," 37–38.

25. Foster and Smith, *Black Religious Experience*, 107.

characteristics: biblical integrity, radical contextuality, systematic engagement, educational change, and programmatic integration,[26] all of which come together to provide a model that takes the Bible outside the church doors to the world while uplifting the Black experience and humanity.

Lora-Ellen McKinney writes that today's church exists in a society in which less value is placed on religion and that the church has moved to the periphery of society. To combat this, Christian formation is even more important, and it must be relevant to Black life in a racist society and church.[27] Since making disciples is the ultimate goal of church, Christian formation becomes a means to that end.[28] As we look at the Black Church, for McKinney, the educated African-centered Christian "is one who grows in their understanding of Christ within the context of a history that includes Africans."[29] Christian education is concerned with the liberation of the soul and with the stabilization and strengthening of congregation members and the external Christian community by enhancing understanding of the African roots of Christianity, the spread of Christianity throughout the diaspora, and the acknowledgment that Christ champions the oppressed and those who want social and spiritual freedom.[30] For older teens and adults who are exploring the Episcopal Church, this could be part of an introductory session.

In assessing the strategies used by Anne Wimberly, Christian formation's relevance assists us in grappling with the realities of life.[31] Key to her strategy is storytelling, which provides a platform to share the liberation story of African Americans and their shared history of slavery while recognizing that God, through Jesus Christ, is on the side of the oppressed as they struggle toward freedom.[32] Hope-building is also an aspect of liberative Christian education, and it is the task of Christian formation to engage members in storytelling as a means of moving toward this hope-building vocation. Students are able to connect what is going

---

26. Foster and Smith, *Black Religious Experience*, 107–11.

27. Lora-Ellen McKinney, *Christian Education in the African American Church: A Guide for Teaching Truth* (Valley Forge, PA: Judson Press, 2003), 9.

28. McKinney, *Christian Education in the African American Church*, 11.

29. McKinney, *Christian Education in the African American Church*, 11.

30. McKinney, *Christian Education in the African American Church*, 183.

31. Anne E. Streaty Wimberly, *Soul Stories: African American Christian Education*, rev. ed. (Nashville: Abingdon Press, 2005), 1.

32. Wimberly, *Soul Stories*, 5.

on in their lives with the everyday stories of the Bible.[33] This means that the stories of the Bible must be interpreted using different cultural lenses.

The storytelling ushers in the concept of story-linking, how our life stories link with the stories of the Bible. Wimberly cautions us that although story-linking has cultural roots in the African and Black experience, it is not always used in churches Blacks attend. In studying the stories of the Bible and telling our stories, we are able to see how the hardships and sufferings of those of an earlier time and God's activity in history are relevant to what is going on in the present age.[34]

The strength of all three strategies lies in the fact that each produces a new consciousness in the learner that is supported by African values and focuses on social justice outside the church. The strategies correct history that has tended to leave Africans and African Americans out of the building and spread of Christianity. This foundation in Africa also makes the learner aware of the history of the Black Church in America and the values brought to the church by those transported here from Africa in chains. These values undergird the Black family today and should be in the forefront of how we engage each other in the church and in the larger community. There is a liberative framework in that God, through Jesus, is concerned with the oppressed, and the three processes provide a mechanism to correct oppressive structures that continue to exist in our society. Education for formation requires action that is congregation-wide, not just with individuals or committees in the church, and the focus is outward; engagement in and of the community in which the church is located is important. Kingdom-building is not only for those in church but also for those outside and surrounding the church building, and an African-centered approach recognizes that community extends outside the church and is key to the personhood of the believer.

The primary, though relatively minor, difference between the three is that Shockley indicates that for his model to be successful in today's church, there must be social action and social engagement in the mission of the church, which, if we model Jesus, is apparent. Wimberly's model differs from the other two in that she specifically uses storytelling and story-linking as a foundation. McKinney uses various tools such as fasting, preaching, teaching, activism, service, music, and geography to link

---

33. Wimberly, *Soul Stories*, 17.

34. Wimberly, *Soul Stories*, 25.

to the Black experience and how that experience is normalized in a racist society and church. While it might seem that the three have slightly different foci, in reality, if one goes beneath the surface of each, all the components are present in each model. It is also important to remember that Shockley offers there is no *Black* Christian formation; rather there is Christian formation conducted within the cultural location of Blacks whose heritage traces back to Africa.[35]

Not everyone is versed in these processes, and it is important to have culturally competent teams that are responsible for the processes. This is not something that can be achieved overnight, and it requires intentionality. There is no one-size-fits-all strategy. Assessing the role our churches play in the lives of our members, we must also expand the term "Christian formation" to include the broader issues of life and those issues of salvation and rites of passage.[36] Willie James Jennings suggests that formation that grounds theological education of all types and reflects Western education is troubled and distorted and that this distorted formation has been with Christianity and the Anglican/Episcopal Church since the first baptism of Africans in Jamestown in 1624. For Jennings, this distortion grounds itself in forming "white self-sufficient men and a related pedagogical imagination calibrated to forming a Christian racial and cultural homogeneity that yet performs the nationalist vision of that same white self-sufficient man."[37] In other words, our formation processes are grounded in whiteness. Until we are able to acknowledge and wrestle with the formation processes that are undergirded by the all-sufficient white man lurking in all our processes, it will be difficult to have formation that celebrates the entire self and to have a vibrant Episcopal faith where members and visitors are able to see and be themselves without conforming to whiteness that is born out of colonialism.[38] The Anglican/Episcopal Church needs to decolonize formation.

While it might be upsetting to some, Jennings offers that our current manner of formation, be it seminary education, church-based rites of passage, or antiracism training, is based on proclaiming a gospel that is useful to the maintenance of the institution—the church, enslavement,

---

35. Foster and Smith, *Black Religious Experience*, 63.

36. Foster and Smith, *Black Religious Experience*, 62.

37. Willie James Jennings, *After Whiteness: An Education in Belonging* (Grand Rapids, MI: Eerdmans Publishing, 2020), 4–7.

38. Jennings, *After Whiteness*, 46–51.

and whiteness. A slave legacy that is embedded in Western education, including the church, is lodged in our educational mindsets in a manner that is subversive, and when we teach, we do so from within a pedagogy of the plantation.[39] To free ourselves from this model of formation, bell hooks writes that there is a choice: we can engage in education or formation that is the practice of freedom, or we can continue to educate or form in ways that reinforce white domination. To practice freedom, we must deconstruct how formation has been traditionally conducted, and in the case of Blacks in a white church, formation becomes an act of resistance.[40] In a society where racism and the threat of death, particularly for Black males, are ever-present, the teacher or instructor becomes a healer. Thich Nhat Hanh calls on students to be active participants in the formation process, a process that emphasizes wholeness and that involves a union of mind, body, and spirit, which enables the student to overcome years of socialization in white society.[41]

Returning to the discussion concerning the three formation models, to empower our Black members, we use Shockley's intentional engagement model.[42] This is a liberative *andragogy*.[43] As a result of participation in this process, those deemed powerless by society and those who feel powerless because of their own personal situations will find their voice and strength to meet the challenges that life presents. As Paulo Freire has written, pedagogy must be forged in concert with the oppressed; therefore, the design of formation processes requires a collaborative effort with those for whom the training is designed.[44]

The process is Afrocentric. Building on the Swahili word *ujamaa*, we focus on the concept of family-hood that is central in assessing the solidarity of African families.[45] As Ronald Edward Peters writes, "'ujamaa'

---

39. Jennings, *After Whiteness*, 82.

40. bell hooks, *Teaching to Transgress: Education as the Practice of Freedom* (New York: Routledge, 1994), 4–11.

41. hooks, *Teaching to Transgress*, 14.

42. Foster and Smith, *Black Religious Experience*, 79. See also Kenneth H. Hill, *Religious Education in the African American Tradition: A Comprehensive Introduction* (St. Louis: Chalice Press, 2007), 121.

43. Foster and Smith, *Black Religious Experience*, 78. I have chosen to use Malcolm Knowles's term *andragogy* (the art and science of teaching adults) as opposed to the more common term *pedagogy* (the art and science of teaching children), although pedagogy is generally used to denote instructional methodology.

44. Freire, *Pedagogy of the Oppressed*, 30.

45. J. Deotis Roberts, "Africentric Christianity and Urban Ministry," in Peters and Haney, eds., *Africentric Approaches to Christian Ministry*, 54.

takes the focus off the materialism of the world and places emphasis on values that are not materialistic."[46] We focus on and value Black members of the faith. We move from a focus on materialism to the strengths that have enabled Black people to survive in a hostile world. The community building is derived from the pattern of self-help that has spread from the Black extended family to Black institutions in the wider Black community that are based on fictive kinship and racial and religious consciousness.[47] The Black family does not rely on blood or marriage; family forms out of necessity. The Afrocentric process is problem posing in which the formation is student centered, developed and organized from the Black member's perspective.[48] Together, the issues facing Black people in society and the church are assessed, and then through Wimberly's story-linking, the curriculum creators arrive at a point where ethical decisions are made by those who will participate in the formation process.[49]

Through story-linking, storytelling, and sharing, negative attitudes and feelings about the Black body can be deciphered and actions taken to return African Americans in the church to a state of wholeness. According to Freire, "the *raison d'être* of liberation . . . lies in its drive towards reconciliation,"[50] a reconciliation that is in Christ Jesus. Participants' collective stories are part of the process from which they and others learn. It is not assumed that the facilitators or the resource persons possess all the information. This process negates what Freire has termed the "banking concept" of education in which those being formed are considered blank slates.[51] Through the church's formation process, Black participants have their humanity affirmed. They also bring a wealth of knowledge to the process, which is an integral part of learning.

High church, low church, and in between all can be African centered in such a way that the humanity of Black Episcopalians is uplifted and celebrated. For most people in our pews, unfortunately, the terms *low*, *broad*, and *high church* have little meaning. Rather, it is what they feel as they experience the worship service and what happens after the final

---

46. Ronald Edward Peters, "Christians Celebrating Kwanzaa: Reflections and Thanksgiving for the African Heritage," in Peters and Haney, eds., *Africentric Approaches to Christian Ministry*, 89.

47. Sadye L. Logan, *The Black Family: Strengths, Self-Help and Positive Change* (Boulder, CO: Westview Press, 1996), 26.

48. Freire, *Pedagogy of the Oppressed*, 90.

49. Wimberly, *Soul Stories*, 55–58.

50. Freire, *Pedagogy of the Oppressed*, 53.

51. Freire, *Pedagogy of the Oppressed*, 53.

dismissal. With an enhanced formation process, the differences in preferences can be shared, and it is important that this be done in extended and intentional formation processes. As John Baldwin offers, "It is unrealistic to imagine that an hour or so a week, and often less than that, of involvement in the liturgical assembly is going to be able to attune people to the value system and way of life to which the Gospel invites all Christians."[52] Without this formational grounding, liturgy has the potential to become rote and mere words. As others have suggested, in assimilating to whiteness Blacks can be attracted to churches and liturgies that are seen as being "less Black," which is grounded in racial self-oppression and lack of knowledge. While differences in liturgical preference are recognized and accepted, Mary Fulkerson and Marcia Mount Shoop remind us that "white-dominant churches especially struggle to live into an incarnational mode of being church."[53] Black bodies are marginalized in typical worship forms as well as in liturgical language most commonly used in white-dominant churches. Worship tends to be more cerebral than embodied. The sermon is more of a lecture than the Word proclaimed.

What Can We Learn from Black Catholics?

What does "Authentically Black and Truly Catholic" mean? In 1984, when ten Black Roman Catholic bishops issued their first pastoral letter, their goal was to answer that question. The letter was issued on the Feast of St. Peter Claver, a patron saint of African Americans. It continued a tradition of questioning or striking back at what was correct or proper that began at the height of the Black Power movement when Fr. George Clements, the African American rector of Holy Angels parish in Chicago, removed the icon of St. Anthony of Padua from the sanctuary, replaced it with a picture of the Baptist minister the Rev. Dr. Martin Luther King Jr., and rededicated a side altar as the "Shrine of St. Martin Luther King Jr." When questioned, Fr. Clements responded that he was acting on the will of his parishioners and the Catholic tradition of *acclamatio populorum*—that Dr. King was a saint because the people had proclaimed him to be a saint even

---

52. Brandt Montgomery, "American Anglo-Catholicism and Black Episcopalians: Integrating the Narrative, Part II: The Witness of Ritualism," accessed August 15, 2021, *https://livingchurch.org/covenant/2019/12/13/american-anglo-catholicism-and-black-episcopalians-integrating-the-narrative-part-ii-the-witness-of-ritualism/*.

53. Mary McClintock Fulkerson and Marcia W. Mount Shoop, *A Body Broken, a Body Betrayed: Race, Memory, and Eucharist in White-Dominant Churches* (Eugene, OR: Cascade Books, 2015), 44.

though the Catholic Church did not recognize him as one. The proper protocol of the Church took a back seat to the need of Black Catholics to lift up one of their own. Holy Angels, a Black parish in a white denomination, began to live into the fact that they were a Black religious community that lived with long-standing Catholic traditions.[54] The bishops' 1984 letter announced, "There is a richness in our Black experience that we must share with the entire people of God. . . . These are gifts that are part of an African past. For we have heard with Black ears and we have seen with Black eyes and we have understood with an African heart."[55]

With the release of that letter, these bishops acknowledged and claimed that there was a uniquely Black way of experiencing the world that led to a distinctly Black way of being Roman Catholic. They acknowledged that Black worship and Black spirituality had a home in the Catholic Church; this spirituality was grounded in an African heritage and contrasted with Western or white traditions. The bishops also acknowledged that while they were truly Catholic, as Blacks, there was a connection with Black Baptists, Methodists, and Pentecostals because of shared history and experiences living as Blacks in this country.[56] Liturgy was to be the tool through which Black Catholics would "come to realize that the Catholic Church is the homeland for Black believers" and that liturgy ". . . should be authentically Black. It should be truly Catholic."[57]

Again, these bishops acknowledged what Black Catholics had embraced during the rise of Black Power that they were Black first and second Catholic, and were inheritors of the Black Church tradition. Black Catholics acknowledged that the Catholic Church in this country was a racist institution, not just because the church was controlled by whites, but also because Black Catholics had "been coerced to conform to white religious norms."[58] Black Catholics reassessed their history and the role of missionaries' evangelism, which Blacks recast as cultural imperialism, and concluded that Blacks had been fed white European Catholicism and had been forcefully removed from their religious cultural heritage.

---

54. Matthew J. Cressler, *Authentically Black and Truly Catholic: The Rise of Black Catholicism in the Great Migration* (New York: New York University Press, 2017), 152–53.

55. United States Conference of Catholic Bishops, "What We Have Seen and Heard: A Pastoral Letter on Evangelization from the Black Bishops of the United States," September 9, 1984, 2.

56. "What We Have Seen and Heard," 15.

57. "What We Have Seen and Heard," 31.

58. Cressler, *Authentically Black and Truly Catholic*, 154.

In acquiescing to white Catholicism, Black Catholics believed they had become "Black-faced white people."[59] They wanted to change this and return to their Black religious heritage while retaining the parts of Catholicism that spoke to them. They wanted to worship in ways that were traditionally Black, and they wanted to uplift Black Power to save the Catholic Church from the sin of white supremacy. Black Catholics critiqued the church's missionary mentality that viewed Black Catholics as foreigners who had to be made good and proper Catholics. This trajectory borrowed phrases from the 1968 Black Catholic Clergy Caucus's statement that identified Catholic missionary strategies as "enlightened paternalism at best and white racism at worst."[60]

Naturally, there was pushback, and at times this opposition came from Black Catholics who saw no difference between Black Catholics and white Catholics; they were just Catholic. As we have seen with those who just want everyone to be Americans, there is a difference, and that difference exists because whiteness determines what "American" or "Catholic" or "Episcopalian" is. As suggested by A. D. A. France-Williams, Anglican theology supports the maintenance of a white male hierarchy.[61] Those who pushed for a distinction wanted Black Catholics to recognize the existence of a distinctive Black Catholicism and their need to become Black Catholics as opposed to being Blacks who happened to be Catholic. Again, this movement found its inspiration in the Black Power movement and rejected the whiteness of the American church. While all religion is about control,[62] Black Catholics wanted to define who they were in the Church and how they would be viewed.

If we accept as Stanley Hauerwas's proposal that "liturgy is social action,"[63] that action taken by the Black Catholic bishops to examine every aspect of the liturgy was correct, because for liturgy to be

---

59. Jamie T. Phelps, "The Theology and Process of Inculturation: A Theology of Hope for African American Catholics in the United States," *New Theology Review* 7, no.1 (February 1994): 5–13.

60. Cressler, *Authentically Black and Truly Catholic*, 155.

61. France-Williams, *Ghost Ship*, 120.

62. All religions exert some form of control over adherents: what to believe, what is appropriate behavior, who is God, whether Jesus is the only way to salvation. There can be food restrictions or garments that must be worn. If people marry outside the tradition, there can be a requirement that the children be brought up in the faith of the believer. Birth control or abortion can be prohibited. In some religions, women are deemed to be subservient to men. There can be penalties for violating the rules, tenets, or doctrines that can include excommunication or shaming.

63. Fulkerson and Shoop, *A Body Broken, a Body Betrayed*, 3.

authentically Black as opposed to merely modified, every aspect had to be examined. It is too easy to simply modify the style of worship to what becomes cultural appropriation as opposed to intentionally incorporating African-ness into the liturgy. Without intentionality, what can occur is a replica of the Eurocentric Christianity without the whites, which is what happens in many Black Episcopal parishes.[64] For these bishops, liturgy had to embrace "the African-American cultural idiom or style in music, in preaching, in bodily expression, in artistic furnishings and vestments, and even in tempo."[65] The result of this intense analysis is that the liturgy of the mass was not changed; it was enhanced, it was enfleshed. Jesus showed up as a brown-skinned Palestinian Jew.[66]

This is a work in progress, because over thirty years later, the question of how to be authentically Black and truly Catholic still exists. Tia Noelle Pratt's work continues what was begun in the 1960s, of identifying and overcoming systemic racism in the Roman Catholic Church and finding how Black Catholics use the liturgy to incorporate both Roman Catholic and Black religious traditions to develop a "cohesive ethno-religious identity."[67] In her work, Pratt has identified three liturgical styles that can also inform Episcopal identity and worship: traditional, spirited, and gospel, which "actively produces Black Catholic parish culture."[68] The first, traditional, reflects the dominant culture of the church; it is Eurocentric, with short homilies and the use of the missalette for hymns. This is easily transferred to the Episcopal Church, where there can be spirited conversations over the proper length of the homily. When translated to the Black parish, this congregation is usually composed of seniors who are not willing to stray from a liturgical style they have either known all their lives or who left another denomination because they wanted something that was not Black. The second style, spirited, allows the Holy Spirt just a little space to enliven the service. African American songs are added to the traditional liturgical style. Finally, there is the gospel liturgical style that more closely

---

64. Whelchel, *The History and Heritage of African-American Churches*, 119.

65. "What We Have Seen and Heard," 31.

66. United States Catholic Conference, "In Spirit and Truth: Black Catholic Reflections on the Order of the Mass," September 1987, 4–30.

67. Tia Noelle Pratt, "Authentically Black, Truly Catholic: Liturgy and Identity in African American Parish Life," *Commonweal*, April 1, 2020, *https://www.commonwealmagazine.org/authentically-Black-truly-catholic*.

68. Pratt, "Authentically Black, Truly Catholic."

aligns with the Black Church. Through preaching, music, and the design and furnishings of the physical church, the lived experience of Blacks in this country comes into play in the worship experience. Again, all three can be found in the Episcopal Church.[69]

The Zaire Mass

In 2019 Pope Francis praised the Zaire Mass, which was celebrated at the Vatican on the First Sunday of Advent. In place of the pipe organ were marimbas, electric guitars, hand shakers, and African and electronic drums. Women in brightly colored African dress processed in instead of men clothed in typical vestments. The liturgy was in the mode of what Tia Noelle Pratt calls "spirited." The liturgy was Roman Catholic but was enhanced with the traditions of the people of the Congo. Pope Francis said, "The experience of the Congolese rite of celebrating Mass can serve as an example and model for other cultures."[70] In addition to lifting up the ancestors and the saints of the Church, the liturgy also includes rituals in the eucharistic rite common to the people. The mass, which was approved for use during Vatican II, found renewed interest because people want their worship experience to be grounded in their lived experiences, their history, and their culture. In an interview for the book *Pope Francis and the Roman Missal for the Diocese of Zaire* the author, Sister Rita Mboshu Kongo, said that the rite is proof that people can pray to God from their own cultural context without altering the unity of the Catholic faith.[71]

This begs the question, Should Episcopal African Americans have their own rite? That was the question asked of Catholics by Nate Tinner-Williams, who was following up on Pope Francis's call for people to enculturate the liturgy. Tinner-Williams believes when cultural groups have their own liturgy, it is not segregation; rather, it shows the catholicity of the church. It shows that various cultures are recognized and embraced. With the 2021 Racial Justice Audit of the Episcopal Church, some might say that perhaps it is time to have an African American rite for those who want it—who *need* it. It just might be a way to evangelize and answer

---

69. Pratt, "Authentically Black, Truly Catholic."

70. Ricardo da Silva, SJ, "Explainer: What Is the Zaire Rite—and Why Is Pope Francis Talking About It Now?," *American Magazine*, December 7, 2020, *https://www.americamagazine.org/faith/2020/12/07/pope-francis-zaire-rite-catholic-church-amazon-239425.*

71. da Silva, "Explainer: What Is the Zaire Rite?"

Rev. Renger's question with, "No, you do not have to leave who you are at the door." It would help the Episcopal Church become less of what Pratt calls "Ultra-white Space."[72] African American rites have been developed by the Union of Black Episcopalians, St. Ambrose Episcopal Church in Raleigh, North Carolina, and other Black parishes; however, these have not been formalized by the Episcopal Church—perhaps they do not need to be. If church is different from the world, has not conformed itself to the world, as the apostle Paul phrased it, shouldn't the church be what Elijah Anderson calls the "cosmopolitan canopy,"[73] a place where one can find respite from the tensions of the world, where the opportunity exists for people who are different to come together and not have their differences cause friction? This is all part of Christian formation. Unfortunately, if the church reflects the racism of society, and insists on a "proper" way of being Episcopalian, it becomes, rather than a place of respite, an ultra-white space where people of color, and particularly Black people, are either not expected or, if present, are marginalized. The Episcopal Church's systemic racism makes it a white space in spite of its claim to catholicity and its call for radical welcome.[74]

Sunday Morning

Formation continues on Sunday morning with the liturgy, the central communal gathering in the church, and if there is to be any marginalization or discrimination, it will first show up there, as Rev. Renger writes.[75] It is more than coming to the door and being told that the "Black church is down the street." What happens on Sunday morning (or any time there is a service) is a major part of the formation process. While there is more research on Black Catholics than Black Episcopalians, that does not mean being more authentic as Black people has not been on the agenda in the Episcopal Church. As indicated by the Racial Justice Audit, more work needs to be done. The 1979 Book of Common Prayer needs to be revised,

---

72. Tia Noelle Pratt, "Why I'm Writing a Book about Black Catholics and Systemic Racism," *Faithfully Magazine*, July 22, 2019, *https://faithfullymagazine.com/Black-catholics-systemic-racism/*.

73. Elijah Anderson, "The Cosmopolitan Canopy," August 2011, *https://fordhamatsdc.files.word press.com/2011/08/cosmopolitan_canopy_eli_anderson_article.pdf*.

74. Elijah Anderson, "The White Space," *Sociology of Race and Ethnicity* 1, no. 1 (2015): 10–21, *https://sociology.yale.edu/sites/default/files/pages_from_sre-11_rev5_printer_files.pdf*.

75. Tia Noelle Pratt, "Racism and Liturgy: Q&A with a Sociologist," *PrayTell Blog*, November 15, 2018, *https://www.praytellblog.com/index.php/2018/11/15/racism-and-the-liturgy-qa-with-a-sociologist/*.

which is a time-consuming and Anglican culture–bound process. Recognizing the trials and tribulations the Church is facing, Resolution A169, presented at the 79th General Convention, called for a revision of the prayer book and to take into consideration the "riches of our Church's liturgical, cultural, racial, generational, linguistic, gender, and ethnic diversity."[76] There is hope in that while we wait for the revision the current prayer book offers flexibility in using the book.[77]

Where do we begin? How do we make the liturgy and the eucharistic service more in tune with African American culture? Optics is everything. From the setting in the sanctuary to the dismissal, messages are being sent and received about who and what is important. When planning the worship service, it is critical to be intentional about the message, which encompasses more than the sermon. The initial introduction to the church provides a first impression, and architecture has meaning. In seminary we studied church architecture and had to visit several parishes. The goal of our visits was to determine "where" God was. Was God high and aloof, with the altar at the far end of the chancel and the cross above, or was God in the center of the people, with the table and cross placed in the center of the nave or sanctuary, in the midst of the people? I was more interested in the stained glass windows and pictures. What color was Jesus? In the biblical stories pictured in the windows, were only white people depicted? Some people look at more than the bulletin while waiting for service to begin. What pictures are used on the bulletin or the electronic screen? How is the environment experienced by people who enter?

Who comprises the altar party? Do those seated in the pews see themselves? Something as simple as the processional can begin the process of transformation. Who carries the cross, and who are the torchbearers? Who are the readers and the intercessors? Everyone—clergy, lay, visitors, regardless of ethnic or cultural identity—should be able to flourish in any setting with the right resources and intentionality. This includes being sure to incorporate our Spanish-speaking and hearing- and visually impaired worshipers into the overall life of the parish. Or we must ask ourselves: Do we have multiple congregations under the same roof?

---

76. Carl MaultsBy, "Enriching Our Worship Music Afro-Centrically," *Music, Liturgy, and Arts*, May 16, 2017, *https://liturgyandmusic.com/enriching-our-worship-music-afro-centrically/*.

77. The Episcopal Church, *Book of Common Prayer* (New York: Church Hymnal Corporation: 1928), 9–10.

Can the traditional liturgy be flexible enough to speak to those who might believe they have been left out even though they sit in the pews? The Beyoncé Mass is the brainchild of Rev. Yolanda Norton, the H. Eugene Farlough Chair of Black Church Studies at San Francisco Theological Seminary. The service is grounded in womanist theology and uses the life and music of Beyoncé, plus dance and preaching, to help Black women "find their voice, represent the image of God, and create space for liberation." Some might think that Beyoncé's music is not appropriate for church, but watch the worshipers, and it is easy to see how the service speaks their language and speaks to them in ways traditional services might not. Rev. Norton also teaches a class on Beyoncé and the Hebrew Bible, in which she uses Beyoncé's music to interpret scripture through a Black feminist and womanist lens.[78]

Biblical Interpretation

Who is preaching the sermon, and how are the biblical texts being interpreted? According to Cheryl Anderson, "There is no such thing as a neutral or unbiased interpretation of scripture. What we have been taught for hundreds of years as the 'correct' interpretations of scripture are based around the needs and worldview of powerful, white, heterosexual western men."[79] Valerie Bridgeman, another womanist biblical scholar, agrees with Anderson and adds that there is no such thing as an objective reading of the sacred texts. Renita Weems continues this idea that we bring to the text an interested reading that is shaped by questions the reader brings to the encounter. While there is nothing inherently wrong with seeing the texts through different lenses, experience has taught us that the dominant white culture tends to be less than enamored with interpretations by those who are not white or European. As Weems has written, white culture is threatened by all other cultures. Religious diversity is threatening; diverse interpretations are threatening. White religious culture is threatened by marginalized persons who claim the right to interpret scripture for themselves. The biblical ethicist Katie Geneva Canon adds, "It is truly written; but is it truly right?"[80]

---

78. See Beyoncé Mass, accessed August 9, 2021, *https://www.beyoncemass.com.*

79. France-Williams, *Ghost Ship*, 154.

80. Valerie Bridgeman, "'How Do You Read It'? A Quest for Faithful Bible Reading in the Face of the Church's Need for Renewal," *https://oimts.files.wordpress.com/2018/11/2018-01-bridgeman.pdf.*

When thinking of how enslavers prohibited Blacks from reading the Bible for themselves, the enslaver must have feared that Blacks would employ a different hermeneutic and learn for themselves the liberative nature of the sacred texts. Esau McCaulley offers that the enslavers' interpretation of the Bible, which they understood to support white degradation of Blacks, was not one of two versions of interpretation, one Black and one white; rather, the interpretations of the enslaver were incorrect. Black interpretation of the sacred texts claimed that God was a liberator and would not condone the enslavement of Black people. While the enslaved related to the Exodus story, they also were drawn to the God of Leviticus, the God who calls God's people to a life of holiness—that is, to live a life dedicated to God.[81] Further, Brian Blount provides support that the enslaver version of interpretation was self-serving and not of God, an interpretation that continued through the centuries. He writes, "Euro-American scholars, ministers, and lay folk . . . have, over the centuries, used their economic, academic, religious, and political dominance to create the illusion that the Bible, read through their experience, is the Bible read correctly."[82] The beauty of Black exegesis is that it has a universal message when accepted via a lens of freedom.

McCaulley uses as an example the story of Mary and Joseph in the Gospels of Matthew and John. Interpreting through the Black lens, we understand the betrothed couple lived under the oppressive gaze of Rome; the empire was an ever-present threat to their existence. Into this mix comes an unplanned and difficult-to-explain pregnancy. We often forget that we know the story; however, the people of the Bible were living the story one day, one situation at a time. The hope of freedom would be knit in her womb, a glorious story for us, but we need to put ourselves in Mary's position during her time. There would be no gender reveal parties for a girl who was pregnant and not married. We know Joseph planned to put her away secretly, although he could have demanded that she be stoned. That is the reality of the story as opposed to the angelic story we have been given. Plus, the focus on the virgin birth is disingenuous to all women because it leaves the purity culture intact. We also know that in the Hebrew, the word *alma* means "young girl," not virgin. If biblical

---

81. Esau McCaulley, *Reading While Black: African American Biblical Interpretation as an Exercise in Hope* (Downers Grove, IL: InterVarsity Press, 2020), 17.

82. Brian K. Blount, *Then the Whisper Put on Flesh: New Testament Ethics in an African American Context* (Nashville: Abingdon Press, 2001), 20.

interpretation is, as McCaulley writes, free to reject the dominance of European interpretation of biblical studies, it must also be free to reject the skepticism that accompanies it. Through the Black experience, Mary represents all who are called to give their very bodies for the cause of liberation and a future that they can only hope will come. For the freedom fighters of the civil rights era and those of the Black Lives Matter movement, Mary can be viewed as "the patron saint of faithful activists who give their very bodies as witnesses to God's saving work."[83]

African Americans have traditionally held the Bible to be the "talking book"—that is, the Bible spoke to them even when they could not read it or even as it was proclaimed incorrectly by the enslavers' ministers.[84] Lisa Bowens offers that Harriet Jacobs interpreted the apostle Paul in a way that made a liar of the enslaver who preached that the African American is not of God. She used her experience as a woman who was subjected to sexual violence to ask the question, "Who are Africans? Who can measure the amount of Anglo-Saxon blood coursing in the veins of American slaves?" Jacobs used Paul's words in Acts 17:26 to challenge the enslavers' assertion that Blacks are less than human and that they were created for the sole purpose to serve whites as enslaved persons. In Acts 17:26 Paul provides evidence that Blacks and whites are one and are equal. But then, Jacobs put a spin on the actions of the enslaver that made him even more of a liar. Black women who have given birth to biracial children provide evidence that Blacks and whites are of one blood. Through the sexual violence—the rape committed upon the bodies of Black women by the white enslaver—the blood has become one. While God has proclaimed it so, the enslaver has made it so, and Paul's words refute the enslavers' claim the Blacks were made for enslavement because of the one-blood doctrine. Jacobs's use of this passage serves to reject slave ideology and critiques the enslavers' predatory behavior. Through rape, according to Jacobs, the enslaver has usurped the Divine's unity of humanity.[85]

Biblical interpretations must continue to be expanded to include more voices that are not white, not Eurocentric. It is not changing the interpretation; rather, it is changing the lens through which the interpretation is filtered.

83. McCaulley, *Reading While Black*, 85–86.

84. Montgomery, "American Anglo-Catholicism and Black Episcopalians."

85. Lisa M. Bowens, *African American Readings of Paul: Reception, Resistance and Transformation* (Grand Rapids, MI: Eerdmans Publishing, 2020), 181–82.

Music

As we continue the formation process, we must return yet again to music. Music is more than an interlude between parts of the service; it *is* the liturgy, the work of the people that moves us through the worship experience. In "Decolonizing Church Music," Yuri Rodriguez discusses the Prosper of Aquitaine and the saying "lex orandi, lex credendi." She suggests that how we pray shapes what we believe, and she asks the question, "Who chooses our *lex orandi*? Who chooses how we pray?"[86]

As with the Beyoncé Mass, no music should be summarily dismissed because some might think it inappropriate as sacred music; after all, different people identify with different types of music. However, who makes the determination that something is inappropriate? I watched a webinar on sacred music for Black History Month. All the musicians were Black and discussed traditional church music. When the moderator indicated that some people might like music with a "little sauce," the expressions on the faces of the musicians were, well, interesting. It was as if music with a little sauce, Black music, was somehow inappropriate as part of the Episcopal liturgy. Yet Black music, from spirituals to contemporary gospel, speak to all kinds of people. Spirituals are more than sorrow songs; they are protest songs. These songs tell the story of Black life in this country. They are songs "born from rhythms of stolen labor." They often contain double-speak and the double-consciousness of W. E. B. Du Bois.[87] They were the enslaved talking back to the enslaver, denying the inhumane treatment and the corrupted teachings of the plantation preacher.

These songs were grounded in what Henry Louis Gates calls "signifying," words that the enslaver approved but were coded and provided an alternate meaning to the enslaved. The coded words were those of rebellion, revolution, and plans to escape.[88] In code, they questioned the faith and ethics of the enslaver. In "All God's Chillun Got Wings," for example, what is really being said is that not everyone who talks about heaven is not going to be there. As we see more and more young people

---

86. Yuri Rodriguez, "Decolonizing Church Music," *Vestry Papers*, July 2021, *https://www.ecfvp.org/vestry-papers/article/933/decolonizing-church-music*.

87. Kaitlyn Greenidge, "Black Spirituals as Poetry and Resistance," *New York Times*, March 5, 2021, *https://www.nytimes.com/2021/03/05/t-magazine/Black-spirituals-poetry-resistance.html?smid=emshare*.

88. Henry Louis Gates Jr., *Signifying Monkey: A Theory of African American Criticism* (Oxford: Oxford University Press, 1988), 44–124.

leaving or not joining churches, the real-world reality of the spirituals might be able to speak to those who feel that their lives don't matter. It is possible that those who seem to have little use for church might actually be looking for a faith that is grounded in truth as opposed to tradition.[89] There is truth in spirituals; they are the cuts through which we bleed.

Spirituals draw from the songs and rhythms of both West Africa and Christian hymns and are unique to the Black experience in this country. These songs also attempt to answer questions about the Black experience lived under oppression: What happens after death? How does one deal with a life that God seems to have destined for suffering? What does freedom feel like? Listen closely and feel the rhythms, and the listener can be transported to the plantation, the cotton fields, the Underground Railroad. Through the music, the listener and the enslaved become one with each other and one with God, who makes a way out of no way.[90] Howard Thurman found that the spirituals keep the history of a people from being erased and provide insight into how an oppressed people made meaning out of a demeaning life. The oppressed people were on a quest to be seen as human.[91] Spirituals also provided a release from that life and provide glimpses of how the enslaved found joy where there should have been none and were able to resist the enslaver's version of reality.

Not So Amazing Grace . . .

Whenever I hear the hymn "Amazing Grace," I cringe. I am a former police officer, and it is a popular hymn sung at funerals for fallen officers. I cringe because its author was a captain of a slave ship. On March 9, 1748, John Newton, his crew, and the human cargo were hit by a vicious storm. The seas were so bad Newton had to be lashed to a beam to survive. The ship, the crew, and its human cargo were almost lost. But all was not lost and Newton expressed his thanks to the Almighty in the words of this popular hymn. He had run from faith and the church in spite of the

---

89. Onleilove Alston, "The Black Presence in the Bible: Uncovering the Hidden Ones," *Sojourner's*, February 19, 2014, *https://sojo.net/articles/faith-action/Black-presence-bible-uncovering-hidden-ones.*

90. Greenidge, "Black Spirituals as Poetry and Resistance."

91. Wyatt T. Walker, *Somebody's Calling My Name: Black Sacred Music and Social Change* (Valley Forge, PA: Judson Press, 1979), 50.

efforts of his mother, but this was a moment of conversion. Yet neither the storm, his near-death experience, nor his conversion were enough to turn him away from his involvement in the trafficking of human flesh. Whenever I hear the hymn played for a fallen police officer, I have to stop singing because the police have been no friends to Black bodies. They, too, traffic in Black bodies. As for Newton, he continued transporting Black bodies as part of the Middle Passage until 1754 when he retired. He was ordained by the Church of England, the denomination that birthed my church, the Episcopal Church, as priest in 1764. Still, he did not repent of his crimes against humanity until after a stroke nearly killed him.[92]

The Rev. Jemonde Taylor, rector of the historically Black St. Ambrose Episcopal Church in Raleigh, North Carolina, has a list of banned songs, songs that if we listen to closely do not lift up Blackness. Many hymns and songs fall into this category, and one is a favorite at Christmas, "O Holy Night." The last verse is problematic:

> Truly He taught us to love one another.
> His law is love, and His gospel is peace.
> Chains shall He break for the slave is our brother,
> And in His name all oppression shall cease.
> Sweet hymns of joy in grateful chorus raise we.
> Let all within us praise His holy name.

For all too many white Christians, the slave is not and was not their brother or sister. Are the chains being broken to free the slave, or does the slave remain in bondage and the free recognize him as a brother? A hymn sung in the Black Church, "I Hear the Savior Say," also lifts up whiteness:

> Jesus paid it all;
> All to Him I owe;
> Sin had left a crimson stain;
> He washed me white as snow . . .

I, for one, refuse to sing any song that washes me white as snow or where whiteness is related to purity or goodness. As we are working with

---

92. Jemar Tisby, *The Color of Compromise: The Truth about the American Church's Complicity with Racism* (Grand Rapids, MI: Zondervan, 2019), 31.

our choirs, do we read all of the verses of the songs we use to see how they might sound to those sitting in our pews who have been hurt by racism, sexism, homophobia, and the rest?

From Gregorian chants, to spirituals, to Jesus hip-hop, music is varied in the Black Church, including the Black Episcopal Church. Our worship services can be greatly enhanced by the inclusion of music from the African diaspora, regardless of who sits in the pews. There is an energy in Afrocentric music that is not present in most Eurocentric music, and again, it is merely a lack of imagination that it does not infuse and enliven our liturgies. Still, in some cases, it can be outright anti-Blackness, particularly when the phrase "it's not Anglican/Episcopal" are used to exclude Black music. When deciding to use Black music, options beyond the hymnal *Lift Every Voice and Sing* exist. Below is a partial list of other hymnals.

African American Heritage Hymnal

Lead Me, Guide Me

Lead Me, Guide Me II

Songs of Zion

This Far by Faith

Total Praise

Wonder, Love, and Praise

Yes, Lord!

Zion Still Sings

In addition to hymnals, Black composers from around the diaspora have written mass settings—for example, "A Mass for a Soulful People" by Grayson Brown and Lena McLin's "Eucharist for the Soul"—and choral music. With a little research, the worship service can be enriched in so many ways.[93] Note, however, that Black music should not be included to check a box, to say, "See? We're multicultural; we're inclusive." Cultural appropriation is an affront. The question must be asked, "Why are we including this music?"

---

93. Carl MaultsBy, "Enriching Our Worship Music Afro-Centrically," *The Weekly Word*, May 16, 2017, *https://liturgyandmusic.com/enriching-our-worship-music-afro-centrically/*.

Holy Communion

How can I at the altar preside?
When it is my body and blood
which are broken?

    —A. D. A. France-Williams, *Ghost Ship*

The communion table is set for us as a place where we come to be welcomed and reconciled to God.

        Mary McClintock Fulkerson and Marcia W. Mount Shoop,
                         A Body Broken, a Body Betrayed

You are invited to sit with the quotation from Anglican priest A. D. A. France-Williams. When Black bodies are broken by the police, by mass incarceration, by poverty, by racism, by adverse health outcomes, from the failure to be seen as human, how can we, with wholeness, preside at the Eucharist? I hear the answer, "Jesus suffered. Jesus is in our suffering." Or we simply ignore and let the opiate that is religion dull us to the contradiction. There are times when misery does not like or want company, even when that company is Jesus. Yes, we can, for a moment, be transported to that place of blissful forgetting, but reality will soon return when we take off the vestments, leave the church, and return to a world that is anti-Black.

The body of Christ is broken—perhaps broken beyond repair—and it has been broken because of us. I often wonder if those in the pews make that connection when the priest raises the host and breaks it during the Eucharist. The body of Christ was broken on Golgotha, and we break it every time every time we celebrate the Eucharist. Do we feel the pain that Jesus felt? Do we recognize that Jesus's body was broken because of us? There, I've said it. It is broken because human beings want Jesus to follow them and not that they want to follow Jesus. It is broken because we, the members, seem to be more concerned with maintaining the institution of the church as opposed to following Jesus—wherever that may take us. The fact that there are denominations and nondenominations and interdenominations is prima facie evidence of the brokenness of the church. *Where it is divided, reunite it.* The fact that there are white churches, Black churches, Latino churches, and churches that cater to the LGBTQIA+ communities reminds us that the church is broken. *Where it is divided, reunite it.* The body of Christ is fractured because of racism, homophobia, xenophobia, and, within individual certain denominations, sexism in the belief that women are not called to preach the loving and freeing gospel of Jesus Christ. *Where it is divided, reunite it.* For some, there is only *one true church*—all others are imposters. In a way, we make a mockery of communion, Holy Communion, or the Eucharist—again another fracture. Can we agree on what it is called when we are to come to the table to be reconciled with Christ? And if we are not reconciled to and with all the members of the body of Christ, then what are we doing when we go to the welcome table, where we know of some people not being welcome or welcomed?

Jesus did not "institute" communion, not in the way we have made it. It was a simple, regular, sabbath, Jewish meal, and Jesus used the opportunity to provide a way that is common to everyone—eating and drinking—a way for those who followed him to remember what he did, how he transformed lives, how he would face down religious and imperial oppression, while he walked this earth. He wanted his followers to remember what he did so they could continue his work. He was preparing them for the work that would follow once he was killed. They were to be evangelists, carrying on with the mission Jesus began—that of transforming the world. With the divisions among us, with the communion table not being welcoming (admit it: not everyone is welcome), not accepting all God's children (admit it: all are not accepted), or not being affirming (admit it: not all churches are affirming), certainly, those who come to the table cannot even pretend to be reconciled with Christ. There are times when it seems that the only way to be the church that is in the image of God, that is the body of Christ, is to dismantle it and begin again because the American and Eurocentric Christian church is built on the shaky ground of racism and other -isms and phobias. The body does not like or care for all its members, and in the Episcopal Church, its members of ebony grace have been less than tolerated; we have been the proverbial thorn in Paul's side whom the church has despised, disparaged, enslaved, segregated, and begrudgingly ordained.

I watch as people line up to receive communion. I used to be one of those people. They look as if they are going to an execution. Perhaps in an attempt to be pious, reverent, their faces are forlorn, unhappy. Some kneel, others stand at the altar rail, waiting for the wafer to be placed in their outstretched hands or on tongues in gaping mouths and then to either sip or dip the wine. This certainly doesn't look like the heavenly banquet, the foretaste of what is to come. It certainly doesn't look like they are happy or joyful that Christ has sacrificed his body for us that we might have life and have it more abundantly. On most Sundays, communion is almost sorrowful. Rarely is there a response to my, "The body of Christ" or "The cup of salvation." Rarely do I hear, "Amen"—yes, this is the body of Christ! Some just walk off and go back to their seats, some cross themselves and then leave and go back to their seats. It seems almost a funeral, that we are killing Jesus all over again, as opposed to taking the body of Christ into ourselves to be energized, revived, and then sent out into the world. There are some churches, thank God, where communion is different.

St. Stephen's and the Incarnation Episcopal Church in Washington, DC, is one of those churches. St. Stephens's has always had a reputation for being different, out there, in the margins with Jesus. In the 1950s, it became the first integrated Episcopal Church in Washington, DC. It was a place where in high school I spent Friday evenings without questions from my parents. Everyone knew St. Stephen's iconic priest, William Wendt, who, it was told, kept a plain wooden casket in his bedroom as a home for blankets until its eventual use was necessary. It was at St. Stephen's where you could become involved in social justice work; it was a hotbed of activity. Gay rights, antiwar demonstrations, civil rights, women's rights—St. Stephen's had it all. When permission was not forthcoming from the Episcopal Church to witness the marriage of John Fortunato and Wayne Schwandt, the entire affair was moved to the First Congregational Church with full attendance by members of St. Stephen's.[94]

At St. Stephen's the Eucharist begins with a procession from the back of the church. As the cross is brought down the center aisle, people leave their seats and fall in behind. Since St. Stephen's is a multiracial, working on becoming a multicultural, church, people who represent the reign of God fall in as the cross leads to the table—a table that looks like a table—in the chancel area, the space in the front of the sanctuary. People fill in around the table. Some kneel, but most stand. (The pre–Covid pandemic mode of standing was shoulder to shoulder.) Children mingle with the adults, some running in and out, as children do, others following the lead of the adults. The words are said, the bread is broken, the cup is lifted; both are shared. There are times when the bread is passed person to person, followed by the cup. Other times, the bread and wine are shared with those at the table by the ministers. People are across from each other; they

---

94. St. Stephen's and the Incarnation Church, "About Us," accessed August 9, 2021, *https://www.saintstephensdc.org/history.*

look at each other. Children sit on the floor before and after they have received. This is a gathering of God's people.

It is a mosaic of races, ethnicities, ages, genders, those who are poor and homeless, and those who are nonbinary. It is not perfect, and there is probably discord among some; however, it looks like what God intended as the Incarnate Christ's body is shared. This is unlike all too many churches where races and ethnicities are of one kind, where those who don't fit into prescribed gender categories are unwelcome, where the seats at the table are reserved for only those who have received the human invitation. People come broken to the table that is supposed to be about reconciliation, and they leave broken as if the body of Christ has lost its transforming power. Holy Communion, the Eucharist as practiced, practiced as a personal act, has the ability to reproduce the brokenness that is in society as opposed to healing it.[95] According to Fulkerson and Shoop, "The wound of race surfaces at the Lord's Table and calls out for acknowledgement and transformation. . . . We gather at the table of a Savior dismembered by violence even as we are invited to remember Him through a curiously sanitized gathering in a seemingly untroubled and safe space."[96]

If we see the Eucharist as formation, a community-making, community-building table that invites us to consider who is on our guest list, one that none of us deserve to be on, we should look to see if our tables reflect the diversity that is God's creation.[97] We live into our mission to be ministers of reconciliation and are empowered to transform this world that we have made a nightmare into the world God wants it to be. We come to this table that is a site of peace building, and we are empowered to break through the hatred that is in us. As we receive the body and receive the wine, as we take Christ into our own bodies, as we become one with him, as we say yes, we must also ask how this act that we do every Sunday and sometimes during the week informs and gives us the resources we need to transform hatred into love.[98] If we are to become ministers of reconciliation, this table becomes the place where once we leave we understand; we

---

95. Fulkerson and Shoop, *A Body Broken, a Body Betrayed*, 2–3.

96. Fulkerson and Shoop, *A Body Broken, a Body Betrayed*, 9, 30.

97. Larry M. Goodpastor, "Holy Communion and the Vision of the Beloved Community," in Thomas Porter, ed., *Conflict and Communion: Reconciliation and Restorative Justice at Christ's Table* (Nashville: Discipleship Resources, 2006), 42–43.

98. Peter Storey, "Table Manner for Peacebuilders: Holy Communion in the Life of Peacemaking," in Porter, ed., *Conflict and Communion*, 57.

know that to be reconcilers, we must first be changed personally and then change the systemic practices of oppression, inequity, and injustice. As the church, the body of Christ, we are called to be instruments of "healing, justice, and peace in the world; striving faithfully for justice and peace is the context in which we realize reconciliation and healing."[99]

I know my interpretation of Jesus instituting communion is off-putting to some. Yes, for Episcopalians, it is a sacrament of the Church; for other denominations, it is called an ordinance and is no less important. Looking at this meal as a regular meal at which Jesus and the disciples ate together reminds many African Americans of the Sunday family meal, another place of formation. Before my grandmother died, those meals would be at her house. When she died, my mother took them over. David Anderson Hooker tells of these meals at his grandmother's table and how he came to see communion differently. He recalls going to seminary, long after these Sunday meals had become a staple of his family's gatherings, and how he and his classmates were tasked with writing about their first communion. "My Catholic, Anglican, and Episcopal colleagues recalled their communion coming on the heels of confirmation. Others recalled communion coming shortly after baptism. For me, my first experience of communion was at my grandmother's table." Hooker goes on to share,

> While the sacramental acts of baptism or confirmation (depending on your tradition) serve as your individual induction into the household of faith, the sacrament of the Lord's Supper is the church's central act of community formation. Similarly, while your birth or marriage into a family may be heralded, the central act of community formation in African American communities is the Sunday family dinner. Participation clearly marks you as a member of the community with the privileges and responsibilities entailed therein.[100]

Hooker writes, and I agree, that his experience with the formalized communion during the worship service "was less profound, less relevant and ultimately less formational in my faith than were my communion

---

99. Stephanie Anna Hixon, "Holy Communion and the Healing of Relationships," in Porter, ed., *Conflict and Communion*, 93.

100. David Anderson Hooker, "Grandma's Supper Is the Lord's Supper: The Experience of African American Fellowship Meals and Sunday Supper as Communion," in Porter, ed., *Conflict and Communion*, 102.

experiences at my grandmother's table and those in the fellowship hall"
after service.[101] It is important to share why Hooker believes this to be:

1. Sunday dinner reclaims the original meal Jesus shared with his
   disciples before the church transformed it into a sacrament. It was
   a shared meal among close friends. After transformation by the
   church, Holy Communion was imbued with both a spiritual and
   worldly dimension. It came to represent the heavenly feast once
   this life ends. The specialness of this meal should not be confined
   solely to a specific moment in the Eucharist, but every time we eat
   or drink, we should recall God's acts of redemption and salvation.
   Imagine how different the world would be if that became a reality.

2. As we sit around the dinner table and share our joys and hurts, we
   reclaim the tradition of oral communication that was key to the
   African religious tradition and history. Sharing these experiences
   around the table while eating connects our life stories to the story
   of the divine in our lives. We share "how we got over."

3. While acknowledging that the Eucharist is the meal of the
   church, when it is shared in the midst of the Black family's Sunday dinner, we continue the tradition of reformation. We recognize that conversion is not an individualistic experience that leads
   to salvation. Rather, sharing the meal in the midst of family lifts
   up the African worldview that we exist because of others. That
   our existence is because of community. "I am because you are
   and because you are, therefore, I am" (Ubuntu) becomes a reality
   around the table. We take that with us when we gather around
   the Lord's table and are joined by all the saints and ancestors who
   continue to lead and guide us through the struggles of life.

4. While the family dinner can be ritual—every Sunday we gather—
   it is not about ceremony. It opens up the opportunity for the Holy
   Spirit to become part of the celebration. Hooker writes, "Ceremony is planned, orchestrated, and does not have a spontaneous
   element; therefore, it lacks the presence and action of the Spirit.
   Ritual, on the other hand, is bound by sacred space and symbols
   and is planned or conceived to the extent that the intentionality
   and purpose are specified; after this point, the Spirit is invoked,

---

101. Hooker, "Grandma's Supper Is the Lord's Supper," 104–5.

and its presence is given reign over the place and participants to accomplish the intended purpose."[102]

5. As we consider communion, could it be that Jesus wanted something common, something people did every day as a means to remember his life and sacrifice? While he broke bread and drank wine, for the Black family it could be sweet tea and cornbread in which Jesus is recognized and continues the process of transformation.[103]

Some will argue against any reinterpretation of the Eucharist and Hooker's invocation of the Black family Sunday meal as the Eucharist; however, we are again reminded of the questions, "Who says?" and "Whose context will be taken as the one truth?" For those who have been oppressed by the church and had its rites, sacraments, and biblical interpretations used to subjugate them, that they find succor in a meal with all God's bounty being shared with family at the table as opposed to standing stiffly and receiving, as one young adult observed, a Styrofoam wafer and a drop of wine, again we ask, "Who says?" And if we leave that formal church table as broken as when we stepped up to it, as Fulkerson and Shoop write, and as we leave, we go back into an oppressive world without any thought given to changing it, then, in my sanctified imagination, I ask, "What is the point?"

Is it possible that we can learn from Bonhoeffer and others and make the Eucharist a revolutionary act? That is, it becomes an act of resistance that shows that evil and the world do not win, that lives can be transformed as they come to the table, that the divided body can be re-membered and we can transcend the boundaries that the world of Caesar forms? For Bonhoeffer, to gather around the table means that we agree to a reorientation to life—that life does not have to be the way it is; that we come to the table to be changed, and this communion becomes a threat to the powers and principalities that deny humanity to God's children. With this focus, when we leave the table, our self-interests are left behind, and private religion is a thing of the past because we know that we have encountered God through the Other. We leave the table understanding that we are part of a countercultural movement that does not primarily focus on an otherworldly experience; rather, our loins are girded for the practice of peace and reconciliation

---

102. Hooker, "Grandma's Supper Is the Lord's Supper," 107.

103. Hooker, "Grandma's Supper Is the Lord's Supper," 104–8.

here on earth. We are now prepared to resist all orders that are not God's desire for God's creation.[104] Bonhoeffer writes, "Our relation to God is not a 'religious' relationship to the highest, most powerful, and best Being imaginable—that is not authentic transcendence—but our relation to God is a new life in 'existence' for others, through participation in the being of Jesus. . . . The church is the church only when it exists for others and we experience this when we come to the table to be transformed.[105] The forces of the world that seek to dominate and cause dissension and hate can only win when the body is dismembered, and if the body remains dismembered when it leaves the table—if the body leaves the table and racism remains—again I ask, "What is the point?"

Baptism

Baptism is the entry rite into the body of Christ, the church of God; it is formation. The enslaved operated under the cover of Christianity when they went to the pond. It was under this cover that vital aspects of Africanity could be practiced even under the eyes of the enslaver. Yorubas, Ashantis, and Dahomeans, as they made their way to the pond, a body of living water, would be reminded of the water ceremony that was steeped in the Bakongo religious ritual. On the plantation, the enslaved revered the Black religious leader because they remembered the authority their African religious leaders held. As they stood at the water's edge, their white robes recalled the Bakongo mythology:

> In the world below, called *mpemba*, land of kaolin, land of all things white, the lordly dead, through powers commensurate with the relative goodness of their life once lived on earth above, lose the impurities acquired in life, acquire a new freshness of existence, and reenter the world.[106]

They carried a staff in the shape of a cross. The points of the cross represented the four movements of the sun, the four corners of the earth, and the four winds of heaven. The horizontal

---

104. Pugh, *Religionless Christianity*, 150–56.

105. Dietrich Bonhoeffer, *Letters and Papers from Prison* (New York: Touchstone Books, 1971), 381–82.

106. Sterling Stuckey, *Slave Culture: Nationalist Theory and the Foundations of Black America*, 25th ed. (New York: Oxford University Press, 1997), 36–39.

branch signified the sea that divides the living from the dead. The staff-cross represented the cycle of death and re-birth, communal renewal, and as the leader carried it, those who remembered the tradition of the Bakongo and the leader were able to mediate the world between the living and the dead. . . . As the initiate is held underwater, the person dies a small death and then is reborn after having communed with the ancestors. Under the cover of Christianity, traditional African religious practices were maintained and passed on.[107]

Thandekele is my South African, my Zulu name. In 1998 I was in South Africa as part of a team providing management training for emerging Black managers. We went on cultural excursions, and on one of these, we visited the Zulu village elders. As we were speaking with residents, we were called by one of the elders and told we were to participate in a naming ceremony. We stood before a dozen tribal elders, and after ten minutes of looking us over and conferring, we were told our new names. Thandekele means "lovable." I love the sound of it. I loved the naming process steeped in eons of tradition that determined my essence—although I'm not sure the elders assessed me correctly, I love my name. I was also named at my baptism, my christening in the Roman Catholic Church. It was the custom that when christened, the child, the initiate, was also given a saint's name. My mother made sure that was done before the ceremony. Gayle Antoinette, I'm named for St. Anthony of Padua. My siblings also have their proper Roman Catholic names, although none of them is Roman Catholic or Episcopal anymore.

Naming ceremonies are important in African cultures. In West Africa, where many of the enslaved called home, names constituted the person's essence—who they were and who they would become. In the 1977 made-for-TV movie *Roots*, we watched the scene as the infant Kunte Kinte was lifted by his father to the heavens with the words, "Behold, the only One greater than yourself," as he was given an ancestral name. On the plantations in this country, it would not be unusual to see a baptism and naming ceremony in all their African glory. Many of the enslaved were from Nigeria, and in Yorubaland, the naming of children was a special ritual because the name represented the time it took for the parents to determine what it would be. The name would often bring the living and the dead closer

107. Stuckey, *Slave Culture*, 18, 38.

together, or it would point the way to the parents' hopes for the child. The enslaver wanted to stamp out any ritual that remembered Africa because in Africa there was freedom. The enslaver feared naming ceremonies and took over the practice of naming or renaming the enslaved because it was another sign that the enslaved was property, not human, and did not have control over their own body.[108] The enslaved were able to get around the enslaver's dehumanizing tactic by giving the child two names: one, a secret name, whispered in the ear by the mother, and the second name that was for daily use and if changed by the enslaver would not matter because it was a designation as opposed to a true name.[109]

It would be a simple adjustment for those who want to incorporate a naming ceremony into the baptismal rite. Referring again to the Rev. Jemonde Taylor of St. Ambrose Episcopal Church in Raleigh, North Carolina, when baptizing infants, if parents approve, they are baptized naked in a very large flower planter that looks like a small pool. When the baby is chrismated, an entire quart of oil is slathered over the baby in an anointing the likes of which most of us have never seen. There are so many ways in which Africanity can be made part of the liturgies of the Episcopal Church. Options should be available for those who desire to celebrate their culture. The Book of Common Prayer indicates that flexibility is permitted, and when the cultures of members and visitors are made a priority in the life of the community, it begins the process of living into the baptismal covenant in which we respect the dignity of all people.

Reflection Questions

1. Describe your church's formation processes; are they liberative or do they further white domination?
2. How was the history of different racial groups that comprise the Episcopal Church taught in any formation process?
3. How do our ancestral stories link with the stories of the Bible?
4. How have you seen yourself in the liturgies of the Church?
5. Are there specific aspects of your culture you would like included in the worship of the Church? What are they?

---

108. Stuckey, *Slave Culture*, 219–20.

109. Lorenzo Turner, *Africanisms in the Gullah Dialect* (Chicago: University of Chicago Press, 1949), 31–43.

In Their Own Words

Male Clergy

Bringing a person of color through the ordination process is different than bringing a white person through the process. We certainly have some overt racism, but I think we have a lot of unexamined general whiteness, for lack of a better word, that has been taken to be normative. We have to learn to break that down. There are a lot of things about the ordination process that require you to have resources, especially monetary resources that you are just not likely to have if you are young or recently graduated college. What if you're young and you have kids? How does that work? Those are things that disproportionately affect us as Blacks. I also think the bigger issue is just basic cultural competency. Who comprises our commissions on ministry (COM)? When I was ordained there were twenty people; there may have been one or two Blacks. There are questions if you're a Black person going through the process, questions that are at least covertly, if not openly, either racist or racially insensitive. I was asked by the COM if I could handle being part of a white church, and I'm like, "I've come from the cathedral."

When you have Latino and Latina folks coming out of Latino congregations, most likely nobody on the COM is from a Latino congregation, so they don't understand. If you're in a Latino congregation, you might not know the '82 hymnal as well because you didn't grow up with it. You may not know the English prayer book as well because you're used to praying it in Spanish. But the commission is going to think, "Oh, you don't know your prayer book. You don't know your hymnal, you don't know your liturgy" because the aspirants are not used to doing the liturgy in English. The same is true with folks from other diverse congregations and contexts as well. You've got to have folks on the COM who reflect not just the diocese as a whole but reflect all the different communities of the diocese and within the Church. We are ordaining not only for the diocese, but also for the Church.

Male Clergy

What do you do when you walk into the parking lot of your parish and you see really nice SUVs and all the bumper stickers—one side says the "Episcopal Church welcomes you" and the other side, "Trump 2020" or "the South will rise again" with a confederate flag. So, you go there and you preach and you preach, "Jesus Christ, crucified." You're told you don't even speak English and are asked where are you from. This is what you deal with sixty years later, what Dr. King said about eleven o'clock being the most seg-regated hour of the whole week. It is true, bar none. It is more true. If you say all are welcome, but not that Negro priest and not his parents and not Brown folk, how are you going to grow? You can't grow like that.

Female Clergy

When I went before the COM, one of the members said, "Let's face it. You're a Black single mother; this process was not created with you in mind." I said, "Well, if you know that, then every one of you around this table has a responsibility to change it." They looked at me, and then they shifted. I remember one of the people said, "You went to EDS, and you lived in their housing?" I responded, "Yes, I liked it. I had a two-bedroom apartment." One of the priests said, "Well, she grew up in the projects on section eight. She probably did love it." And I was like, "Lord, hold on." The rector at my previous church asked me how I could afford to wear locs, because middle-class Black women couldn't afford to pay that much money to have their hair done.

Female Clergy

One of the problems with parishes in the Episcopal Church is that folks like it their way. But it has a negative effect of chasing people away. I was talking to a friend of mine, and he says, "You know, they don't want the young people, but when you die, if the young people aren't there, the church is gone." We do have church, the twenty- and thirty-year-olds are finding church. It's just not a building. It is Black Lives Matter, it's BIPOC yoga communities, it's dinner church. It is other communities of support to nurture their soul. They're having the same exact conversations we would have in the church, but they're not in the church.

Female Clergy

Question: How long do you think you'll be able to stay?

Answer: Only the Lord knows.

SENDING WORDS

The longer I live, the less I care about orthodoxy and the more I care about love, healing, and the people with whom I'm honored to share life's journey.

—Rev. Mike Kinman

I have little interest in the doctrinal bells and theological whistles that drive so much of Christendom today.

—Rev. Obery Hendricks Jr.

Can I be Black and Episcopalian?

I'm not sure.

I understand the technical aspects of being Episcopalian, and if that is what it takes, then I'm Episcopalian. I've checked all the boxes, including becoming ordained with all that requires. I still have the same problem I had in seminary with the profession of faith, the Nicene Creed, so there are times when I stand mute. When I am able to design liturgy in the way that is uplifting to others and me and in a way in which my culture is recognized, then I'm Black and Episcopalian. When I am able to go beyond the church and engage in the transformative mission of Jesus, then I'm Black and a follower of Jesus, and it doesn't matter if I'm Episcopalian. Jesus doesn't care if I'm Episcopalian.

What does matter is whether the Episcopal Church cares about the Black people in its pews to make all the resolutions and pastoral letters and initiatives (Becoming Beloved Community, for example) a reality instead of waiting until God's time, instead of using the words, "It will take more than our lifetimes." It just might take more than the lifetimes of some, but let's not give ourselves an excuse not to be committed to changing life here and now. God did not create racism; people did, and people can end it. The world as we experience it was created by human beings, and human beings can and must change it. If not, then we are condemning future generations to the soul-stealing infection that is racism, and the Church should not be involved in passing on that legacy. I'm sure I don't want that listed in my book of life.

Other things can be done as we work toward the elimination of the -isms and phobias in the Church. First, be truthful about how people have been treated and continue to be treated. Make brave space for people to tell their stories without retribution. Make sure every curriculum in each seminary has as complete a history of the Episcopal Church as possible, knowing that it will be updated as we learn more. Provide the opportunity for nonwhite, noncisgendered people to write and have their histories included. If not, we will always have history told by those who have access.

Second, challenge single-race churches to expand their base through active evangelism. Ask the question, "Why are you so white, Black, or Latinx?" and be prepared for the answers. We can add questions to the list. This has a proviso: it must not be assumed that white congregations are better and that nonwhite congregations should be absorbed by them if merging is a consideration.

Third, ensure that people in the pews and those who visit see themselves in the liturgy. Be intentional, be authentic. Invite those who are different from the majority of the congregation to assist in designing liturgy. Invite them to preach, to sing, to read—not as a show but with a view toward real inclusion. Assess the art used in churches. What color is Jesus and others whose stories are told in our stained glass windows?

Fourth, rethink formation. Who or what are we forming and for what purpose? If we are forming disciples of Jesus, we need to focus on his mission on earth and how he challenged the powerful. We need to prepare to stay a while at the foot of the cross and not rush to Easter. We need to remember, as the justice advocate Fr. Daniel Berrigan offered, "If you're going to follow Jesus, you need to get used to looking good on wood." We are going to have to go through the cross to change this world. And as we begin the formation process, be sure to include the history of the Episcopal Church, all of its history so people can make an informed choice of whether they want to become part of this tradition.

Fifth, when it comes to creeds and doctrines, we must ask their real purpose and if they need to be revisited. After all, those who created them were human beings like the rest of us and, like us, were attempting to figure out what faith looked like in practice. What if we focused on the two commandments Jesus gave us, to love God and love each other as we love ourselves?

Sixth, we have learned during the Covid-19 pandemic that church is not the building. We knew that before, but we have an irrational love affair with buildings. We like to keep God cooped up in boxes. We know that mission is what takes place after the dismissal. How can we be a true blessing to the communities, the hurting communities, that surround us? Consider repurposing the buildings, especially if the congregation no longer fills the pews. God let the Hebrews wander in the wilderness for forty years until the naysayers and "yes, but" folks died out and a newer, younger generation was able to enter the promised land. As we look at our congregations, it won't take forty years, and, as we look back, the Joshua generation won't be there to lead us into a newer future if they are not with us now.

Seventh, for a second time, create brave space for all the hurting people who are in this Church to tell their stories, to tell their truth without repercussion. The trauma needs to end. The white dominant culture, which includes the Episcopal Church, must stop inflicting spiritual violence on Black bodies by perpetuating our trauma and silencing our voices. We are more than Anglican, and the voices, the experiences, the traditions enhance the church.

Eighth, provide resources and support for people of color who serve in all-white or majority-white congregations. Do not assume that ordination provides a special layer of protection against racism. What about support for whites who serve Black or other minority congregations? Unfortunately, we are used to having whites in positions of authority, and all too often, we acquiesce to whiteness. They don't need the resources and support; we do.

Ninth, in the words of the Rev. Jemonde Taylor, uncouple whiteousness, that everything white is right and in right relationship with God.

When Presiding Bishop Michael Curry preaches, it is always about love: the love of Jesus, the love of God. I always find myself asking, "What does the love of which he preaches look like?" It looks like the things I've listed, and my list is not exhaustive. Church is not a place where we come to hide from the world; we come to be strengthened to deal with the world we have created. If we put what I've suggested into action, that is what love looks like. If we become serious about being disciples of a Palestinian Jew, that is what love looks like. If we create space where people can bring their whole selves to the Church, in whatever form that might be, bring their whole selves to the table, to the welcome table, without fearing rejection, that is what love looks like. If we can join Jesus in his transformative mission to change the world, that is what love looks like, and then, maybe then, I can be Black *and* Episcopalian.

ACKNOWLEDGMENTS

I wish to thank my Episcopal clergy and lay colleagues who provided insight, who shared their lives. To my mentor, the Rev. Vincent Powell Harris, I will forever be indebted. As I was navigating the ordination process, I was asked what type of mentor I wanted, and I answered, "One who pushes the envelope." Rev. Harris continues to do so, and he pushes me to be better in this vocation I chose not for myself. To the folks at Church Publishing, particularly my editor, Milton Brasher-Cunningham, I owe a debt of thanks and gratitude.

I must also make a confession. In my first book, *Preaching Black Lives* (*Matter*), I "confused" the Rev. Dr. Pauli Murray with the Rt. Rev. Barbara C. Harris. I wrote that Pauli was the crucifer at the ordination of the first women as priests in the Episcopal Church. She was not; the crucifer was Barbara. Don't ask the question, because I have no answer. As I write this, I see the picture in my mind, and it is of Barbara with the cross. These are two greats who paved the way for me and on whose shoulders I stand. I do know I was reading books about both as I was writing, and I apologize. It will never happen again.